Marvin Frem

Historic Inns
of Quebec

Fitzhenry & Whiteside

Fitzhenry & Whiteside Limited
Markham, Ontario

Canadian Cataloguing in Publication Data

Fremes, Marvin, 1923-
  Historic Inns of Quebec

Includes index.
ISBN 0-88902-970-9 (bound) — 0-88902-734-X (pbk.)

1. Hotels, taverns, etc. — Quebec (Province) —
Directories.   2. Restaurants, lunch rooms, etc. —
Quebec (Province) — Directories.   I. Title.

TX910.C2F74 1984   647'.94714   C84-098847-8

Editor: Frank English
Copy Editor: Claire Côté
Design: David Shaw
Typesetting: Jay Tee Graphics Ltd.

Printed and bound in Canada

Contents

Eastern Townships and Beauce / 58

Introduction

As a Canadian and a native of Ontario, I have always felt the greatest fascination for the Province of Quebec.

Because its history stretches back over 450 years, more than twice that of my own province, and because of the great respect for their history shown by Québécois, I stand somewhat in awe.

I hope that you will catch my enthusiasm for its history, as commemorated through its historic inns, as much as I did. A word about the so-called language problem. Francophones have been speaking French in Quebec for over 400 years and are likely to continue speaking it for a long time. They are more comfortable speaking French than English (though many are fluently bilingual). As an Anglophone, I have had business dealings in Quebec and have travelled there for many years and can truthfully say that I have never had a problem even though I have limited facility in French. I treat the people and their language with respect, which is what anyone should do.

By using such simple phrases as "Parlez-vous anglais?" or "Je ne peux pas parler français," you can indicate your weakness in the language and, I am sure, open the way to helpful cooperation.

With the exception of two places, all the inns are at least 75 years old. Château Montebello, built in 1937 as it stands, is such an unusual complex that it is a worthwhile entry. In addition, the story surrounding its rapid construction makes it doubly unusual. Auberge St-Denis in St-Saveur has a rather unusual, wartime story to tell and I thought it should be included.

It is a common perception that inns are essentially small and, for the most part, this is true. But some, such as Château Montebello, Ritz-Carleton, Domaine St-Laurent, etc., are quite large. However, that history is so fascinating that I feel that they must be included.

For your convenience the province has been divided into six regions complete with maps. Also a complete alphabetical index is listed at the back of the book.

This book would not have been possible without the gracious cooperation of Lionel Poulin, Quebec Department of Industry and Tourism. His help and guidance were invaluable. Also, I want to express my appreciation to the Regional Directors of Tourism throughout the province for their help. Also, I would like to acknowledge the assistance of Quebecair in my Gaspé travel arrangements.

Finally, to eliminate confusion over ever-changing prices I have set up the following price categories.

	Accommodations	Dining
Very inexpensive	$25 - $50	
Inexpensive	$50 - $75	$5 - $10
Moderate	$75 - $100	$10 - $15
Expensive	$100 plus	$15 plus

In conclusion, I have made no attempt to pass judgement on the quality of accommodations or dining. My intention simply is to offer interesting historical alternatives to the traveller.

No book such as this can ever be complete. If, in your travels, you come upon an inn worthy of inclusion, please send the information to my attention at Fitzhenry and Whiteside Limited, 195 Allstate Parkway, Markham, Ontario, L3R 4T8.

Useful Phrases

FOR SELECTING A MEAL

Soup ... chicken soup ... clear soup ... fish soup ... Toast ...
Soupe ... soupe au poulet ... consommé ... bouillabaisse ... Rôtie ...

Tomato juice ... prune ... apple ... grape ...
Jus de tomate ... pruneaux ... pomme ... raisin ...

Hard-boiled eggs ... soft-boiled eggs ... fried eggs ... scrambled eggs ...
poached eggs ...
Oeufs durs ... oeufs à la coque ... oeufs frits ... oeufs brouillés ... oeufs pochés ...

Beef ... filet mignon ... sirloin ... roast beef ... beef stew ...
hamburger ...
Boeuf ... filet mignon ... surlonge ... rôti de boeuf ... ragoût de boeuf ...

Mutton ... mutton stew ... lamb ... leg of lamb ... veal ... breaded
veal chops ...
*Mouton ... ragoût de mouton ... agneau ... gigot d'agneau ... veau ... côtelettes de
veau panée ...*

Pork chops ... pig's knuckles ... cold pork ... sausage ... ham ...
Côtelettes de porc ... jarrets de porc ... porc froid ... saucisse ... jambon ...

Cold cuts ... kidneys ... brains ... liver ... rabbit ...
Viandes froides ... rognons ... cervelle ... foie ... lapin ...

Chicken ... turkey ... young stuffed turkey ... duck ... duckling ...
goose ...
Poulet ... dinde ... dindonneau farci ... canard ... caneton ... oie ...

Steak ... meat pie ... frog's legs ...
Steak ... tourtière ... cuisse de grenouilles ...

Fish ... lobster ... oysters ...
Poisson ... homard ... huitres ...

Mackerel ... pike ... salmon ... shrimp ... tuna ... walleye ... trout
...
Maquereau ... brochet ... saumon ... crevettes ... thon ... doré ... truite ...

Eel ... haddock ... mussel ... snails ... herring ... cod ...
Anguille ... aiglefin ... moules ... escargots ... hareng ... morue ...

Lettuce ... cucumber ... spinach ... green peas ... green beans ...
Laitue ... concombre ... épinards ... petits pois ... haricots verts ...

Cabbage ... cauliflower ... mushrooms ... carrots ... tomatoes ... beets
...
Chou ... chou-fleur ... champignons ... carottes ... tomates ... betteraves ...

Onion ... asparagus ... potatoes ... rice ... radishes ...
Oignon ... asperges ... pomme de terre ... riz ... radis ...

French-fried potatoes ... mashed potatoes ... boiled potatoes ...
Patates frites ... purée de pommes de terre ... patates bouillies ...

Sauerkraut ... pickles ... cheese ... pancakes ... tea cakes ... ice cream
...
Choucroute ... cornichons ... fromage ... crêpes ... petits fours ... crème glacée ...

WHEN TRAVELLING BY CAR

How far is it to Montreal? ... ?
À quelle distance sommes-nous de Montréal? ... ?

Are we on the road to Montreal? ... ?
Sommes-nous sur la route de Montréal? ... ?

Is there an expressway to Montreal? ... ?
Y a-t-il une autoroute pour Montréal? ... ?

Are there toll charges?
Y a-t-il des postes de péage?

Do I turn left, right, or go straight at the next crossroads?
Dois-je tourner à gauche, à droite, ou aller tout droit, au prochain carrefour?

Where is the nearest ... ?
Où se trouve ... la/le plus proche?

policeman ... fire station ... dentist ... doctor ... hospital ...
le policier ... la caserne de pompiers ... le dentiste ... le médecin ... l'hôpital ...

Can you show me the best route on this map?
Pouvez-vous m'indiquer la meilleure route sur cette carte?

Where are we right now?
Où sommes-nous actuellement?

Where does this road lead?
Où conduit cette route?

How many miles to the next town?
À quelle distance sommes-nous de la prochaine ville?

How long will it take us to get to Sherbrooke?
Combien de temps faut-il pour se rendre à Sherbrooke?

IN TOWN

Where is the shopping district?
Où se trouve le centre commercial?

How do we get to St. Catherine Street?
Comment se rendre à la rue Ste-Catherine?

Is there a good restaurant nearby?
Y a-t-il un bon restaurant près d'ici?

drug store ... service station ... garage ... bank ...
la pharmacie ... le poste d'essence ... le garage ... la banque ...

telephone ... bakery ... swimming pool ... beach ... church ...
le téléphone ... la patisserie ... la piscine ... la plage ... l'église ...

parking lot ... grocery store ... hardware ... newsstand ... barber ...
*le terrain de stationnement ... l'épicerie ... la quincaillerie ... le kiosque à journaux ...
le barbier ...*

POINTS OF INTEREST

Is there an art gallery? ... a museum? ... a zoo?
Y a-t-il une galerie d'art? ... un musée? ... un zoo?

historic sites ... parks ... campgrounds ... trailer park
des lieux historiques ... des parcs ... un terrain de camping ... pour roulottes

Church ... Presbyterian ... United ... Roman Catholic ... a synagogue
Une église ... presbyterienne ... unie ... catholique ... une synagogue

Is there a souvenir shop? ... a department store? ... a liquor store?
*Y a-t-il une boutique de souvenirs? ... un magasin à rayons? ... un magasin de la
Société des Alcools?*

Is there a concert hall? ... a moving picture theatre? ... a wax museum?
Y a-t-il une salle de concerts? ... un cinéma? ... un musée de cire?

Are there any organized tours? ... by bus? ... by taxi?
Y a-t-il des visites organisées? ... en autobus? ... en taxi?

Are any boat tours available?
Y a-t-il des excursions en bateau?

Two tickets, please.
Deux billets, s'il vous plaît.

Where is the nearest post office? . . . restaurant? . . . hotel? . . . service
station? . . . Anglican church? . . . clothing store? . . . florist?
*Où se trouve le bureau de poste le plus proche? . . . le restaurant? . . . l'hôtel? . . . le
garage? . . . l'église anglicane? . . . le marchand de confections? . . . le fleuriste?*

AT THE INN

What are the rates?
Quels sont vos prix?

A single room with bath, please.
Une chambre avec bain, pour une personne, s'il vous plaît.

Have you a room with twin beds? . . . a double bed?
Avez-vous une chambre avec lits jumeaux? . . . un lit double?

What credit cards do you accept?
Quelles cartes de crédit acceptez-vous?

Do you accept travellers' cheques? . . . personal cheques?
Acceptez-vous les chèques personnels? . . . les chèques de voyage?

Is the room quiet?
La chambre est-elle tranquille?

I want a front room . . . a rear room.
Je veux une chambre à l'avant . . . à l'arrière.

Where do I register?
Où dois-je m'inscrire?

I am staying only one night . . . several nights.
Je ne vais rester qu'une nuit . . . je vais rester plusieurs nuits.

May I speak with the manager, please . . . with the room clerk?
Puis-je parler au directeur, s'il vous plaît . . . au préposé à la réception.

Room service, please.
Le service, s'il vous plaît.

There is no toilet paper . . . soap . . . hot water . . . heat . . . electricity.
Il n'y a pas de papier de toilette . . . de savon . . . d'eau chaude . . . d'électricité.

I want some towels ... ice cubes ... soft drinks.
Je veux des serviettes ... des cubes de glace ... des boissons gazeuses.

Can I have my suit cleaned ... my dress ... my sweater?
Puis-je faire nettoyer mon complet ... ma robe ... mon chandail?

Is there a dining room in the hotel?
Y a-t-il une salle à manger dans l'hôtel?

Do you serve breakfast? ... lunch? ... dinner?
Servez-vous le petit déjeuner? ... le déjeuner? ... le dîner?

At what time must I check out?
À quelle heure dois-je libérer la chambre?

AT THE SERVICE STATION

Fill the tank with regular ... super (extra) ... unleaded.
Faites-le plein avec l'essence ordinaire ... de l'essence super (extra) ... sans plomb.

My battery is dead.
Ma batterie est à plat.

Please check the antifreeze.
Vérifiez l'antigel, s'il vous plaît.

How much will this cost?
Combien cela coûtera-t-il?

Do you accept this credit card?
Acceptez-vous cette carte de crédit?

Please check the oil ... battery ... radiator ... transmission.
Verifiez l'huile ... la batterie ... le radiateur ... la transmission, s'il vous plaît.

Please change the oil and grease the car.
Veuillez vidanger l'huile et graisser la voiture.

I have a flat tire.
J'ai un pneu crevé.

Where are the washrooms?
Où sont les toilettes?

The motor will not start.
Le moteur ne veut pas démarrer.

OTHER USEFUL EXPRESSIONS

Mister ... Mrs ... Miss ... boy ... girl
Monsieur ... Madame ... Mademoiselle ... jeune homme ... jeune fille

Yes ... no ... please ... thank you
Oui ... non ... s'il vous plaît ... merci

Now ... earlier ... sooner ... later ... today ... tomorrow ... next week
Maintenant ... plus tôt ... plus tôt ... plus tard ... aujourd'hui ... demain ... la semaine prochaine

Good morning ... good day ... good afternoon ... good evening ... good night ... goodbye
Bonjour ... bonjour ... bonjour ... bon soir ... bonne nuit ... au revoir

I don't understand.
Je ne comprends pas.

How do you do? ... How are you?
Comment allez-vous? ... Comment allez-vous?

Very well, thank you.
Très bien, merci.

What's your name? ... Glad to know you.
Comment vous appelez-vous? ... Enchanté de vous connaître.

I don't speak French very well.
Je ne parle pas très bien le français.

Speak slowly, please ... Please repeat.
Parlez lentement, s'il vous plaît ... Voudriez-vous répéter, s'il vous plaît.

Pardon me.
Excusez-moi.

I don't know ... I cannot.
Je ne sais pas ... Je ne peux pas.

It doesn't matter ... It's not important.
Cela ne fait rien ... Ça n'a pas d'importance.

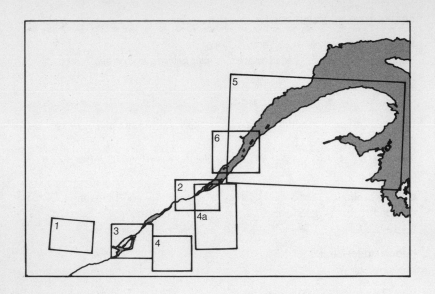

Ottawa Valley

The Ottawa River was one of the "Roads of Empire" during the 17th and 18th centuries. Champlain and those who followed him — fur traders and later lumberers — used the Ottawa as a highway to the interior. Thus, one of the inns (Symmes) in Aylmer was once a fort owned by the North West Company to protect its fur-trade routes.

Later a large immigration of Irish came to the area and dominated the lumber trade. Now many people speak of their ancestors as being both Irish and French.

Today the area is dominated by the National Capital Region, which includes the capital area of Ottawa, along with Gatineau Park outside Hull (Mackenzie King's Kingsmere is located there). The Gatineaus are famous for excellent skiing and summer sports, and there are many fine resorts and inns throughout the area.

Ottawa Valley

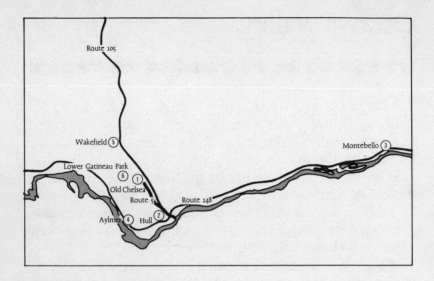

1 Café l'Agaric
2 La Ferme Columbia
3 Le Château Montebello
4 Le Restaurant l'Hôtel Symmes
5 Maison Earle House
6 Mooreside Tearoom and Museum

Café l'Agaric
Old Chelsea, Québec
J0X 2N0

Innkeeper: Paul Throop
Telephone: 819-827-3030
Credit Cards: MasterCard, Visa
Facilities: Dining. Fully licensed.
Open year-round. Closed
Mondays. Hours: 9 a.m. - 8 p.m.

L'Agaric has an unusual name and an unusual background. L'Agaric is the name for a type of wild mushroom grown in the area. Enough are picked in the summer to last the year. The method of preserving them is to dry them and keep them in air-tight jars. They add a delicious flavour to the dining at L'Agaric.

L'Agaric is deeply embedded in the history of the Gatineau Hills. In the early 19th-Century timber era, it was the tollkeeper's house for the Gilmour Mills. When timber gave way to hydro-electric power, the Gatineau Power Company bought the property as part of its effort to harness the turbulent Gatineau River as it plunged down to the Ottawa River. All buildings were removed including this gatehouse which was eventually moved to Old Chelsea. One can imagine what a sight it must have been — this little green cottage moving down the road on a precarious little rig. Now it is safely and (I hope) permanently settled in Old Chelsea, serving its delightful and unusual meals.

Though prices are modest, very unusual dishes are served . . . Heart of Palm Tree with cheese, Brain of veal in mustard sauce, Guinea hen with sake (!).

Directions: Proceed north from Hull on Route 5 for 20 kilometres (12 miles) to Old Chelsea.

La Ferme Columbia

376, boulevard St-Joseph
Hull, Québec
J8Y 3Y7

Innkeeper: Adolphe Calbert
Telephone: 819-776-6484
Credit Cards: All major cards
Facilities: Dining. Open Monday to Saturday, all year. Fully licensed. Lunch: 12-2:30 p.m. (Monday to Friday). Dinner: 6-10:30 p.m.

This fine house was originally the home of Philemon Wright, a Massachusetts emigrant who located in the area around 1800. This industrious entrepreneur was the pioneer of the Ottawa Valley timber trade, rafting lumber down the Ottawa and St. Lawrence rivers to Montreal and Quebec City. Through the use of generous grants of Crown Land, he also established what was to become the City of Hull. As the prominent citizen of the area, he sat in the Assembly of Lower Canada from 1830 to 1833.

The house remained in the family until the early 1890s when the entire farm property was leased to the Ottawa Gulf Club. The lease included a clause which made the Club responsible for injuries to cattle still roaming the property, as well as a barn which served as a hazard to one of the course greens.

The house is now prized as one of the few remaining examples of the most highly developed stage of Canadian Georgian design.

After working up a voracious appetite from a brisk skate on the

4

Rideau Canal in neighbouring Ottawa, my daughter and I enjoyed a relaxing dinner in the 1983 *Travel Holiday Award* dining room.

The à la carte menu offers traditional Quebec fare as well as continental French dishes like foie gras Strasbourg, frog's legs Provençale and Chateaubriand. Duck, quail and veal, served variously, are house specialties. We enjoyed the grilled sirloin steak with Béarnaise sauce and the rack of lamb, Dijonnaise. *Prices:* expensive.

Le Château Montebello

392, rue Notre-Dame
Montebello, Québec
J0V 1L0

Innkeeper: Société Hôtelière Canadien Pacifique
Telephone: 819-423-6341, 1-800-268-9420
Rooms: 204, with bath
Rates: expensive
Credit Cards: All major cards
Facilities: Dining, tennis, golf, swimming (indoor and outdoor), bicycling, cross-country skiing, curling, sauna.

It's difficult to know where to begin to describe this magnificent resort/convention complex on the Ottawa River just a few miles from Hull. Though Château Montebello is barely 50 years old, its origins are deeply rooted in Quebec history.

The story really begins in 1674, when Bishop Laval was given the seigneury by the West Indian Company. It was subsequently sold to Louis-Joseph Papineau, the leader of the 1837-38 rebellion in Lower Canada. He began to settle and develop the property, and today his manor house stands a few yards from the Château, a gracious monument to our colourful past. It is open to the public for guided tours.

In 1930, in the astoundingly short space of four months, this two-hundred room hexagonal complex became the Seigneury Club, opening on July 1. A small city had to be created to support the construction of this impressive log structure in such a short time. Special roads and a rail spur were built and 3500 men were employed. Gastin Periard, a hotel employee, remembers his family putting up temporary cots in their home to house and feed them. They came from all over the continent to get work in those first few Depression

months. During that first year locals called it "Le Boom" and one can easily imagine what a boost it must have been to the local economy.

Gastin fondly remembers looking forward each year to greeting the same families as they returned to the Seigneury, and watching the children as they grew up.

In 1973, the Seigneury Club was sold to the Canadian Pacific which now is operating it as a public hotel/resort.

You have only to step into the foyer and view the imposing hexagonal stone fireplace rising four floors to the roof, to know that you are entering a truly unusual building. Claude Pranno, Director of Sales, took us on a tour showing us the very simple, yet elegant corner VIP suites as well as the regular rooms.

My daughter and I enjoyed Sunday brunch in the Main Dining Room. Rising two floors and surrounded by a viewing gallery, it suggests a formal grandness of another era. Dress is casual but the brunch is another story. Two tables, running almost the full width of the dining room are laden with all sorts of delectable foods including whole boiled salmon, roast beef, ham and, of course, the famous tourtière (pork pie). This buffet is expensive but very good.

The dinner menu is also served in grand manner. Starting off with the indispensable split-pea soup, canapés and spinach turnovers, one proceeds to a main course of Salmon steak, Beef Stroganoff, or Sirloin steak to mention only a few. *Prices:* moderate.

If breakfast and lunch appeal on a simpler level, the Café Habitant is a delightful change. During the summer, guests can sit out on the patio overlooking the Ottawa River. In the winter, the Café overlooks the skaters on the rink just outside.

Directions: Take Route 148 east, 66 kilometres (40 miles) from Hull to Montebello.

Le Restaurant l'Hôtel Symmes

1, rue Front
Aylmer, Québec
J9H 4W8

Innkeeper: Ronald Lefebvre and Nick Orfanos
Telephone: 819-684-2211
Credit Cards: All major cards
Facilities: Dining. Fully licensed. Open year-round, Tuesday to Sunday. Lunch: 12-3 p.m. Dinner: 6-10 p.m. Sunday brunch: 11 a.m. - 3 p.m.

What is now a fine restaurant on the banks of the Ottawa River began as an 18th-Century fort of the North West Company built to protect its fur-trading routes. Later, Philemon Wright, the founder of Hull, converted it into a general store. His nephew, Charles Symmes, founder of Aylmer, then developed it as a hotel serving the stage-coach routes out of Hull in the 1830s. Until a few years ago, the building had been allowed to degenerate almost to ruin. Then in 1980, the Outaouais Development Corporation completely rebuilt it.

L'Hôtel Symmes is now a tribute to the grace and charm of its hosts, Ron and Nick. They have even leased the main floor to a craft and gift shop, Le Grenier des Artisans. Here, one can browse before or after dining. The second-floor room is done in traditional French-Canadian style, while the third (my favourite) is decorated in cool green colours offset by sharp white napery — all underneath a gabled ceiling.

7

Nick was particularly ecstatic about the summer dining. His eyes fairly twinkled when he spoke of dining on the verandah, barbecuing on the lawn, or even taking one's dessert and coffee out to watch the various sail and motorboats returning home at sunset from their day's outing.

Nick tells me his favourite dish, and one that is quite popular, is the Black Pepper steak decorated with peppercorns of many colours — a treat for the eye as well as the palate. Other selections include Filet of pork, French-Canadian style and Lamb chops with a "taste of the orchard." *Prices:* moderate.

There is an interesting note appended to the menu which reads:

The Table d'Hôte allows our chef to exercise his creative genius in offering certain seasonal specialties, such as quail, pheasant, goose, rabbit, deer, buffalo.

In addition, one can select Sirloin or Filet of beef, Beef Medallions, Calf sweetbreads and Duckling roasted with citrus fruit and apples.

Directions: Take route 148 for about 15 kilometres (9 miles) west from Hull and follow rue Principale to the riverfront.

❧❧❧❧❧❧❧❧❧❧❧❧❧❧❧❧❧❧❧❧❧❧

Maison Earle House

Wakefield, Québec
JoK 3Go

Innkeeper: Bob Laflamme
Telephone: 819-459-3273
Credit Cards: All major cards
Facilities: Dining. Fully licensed.
Open daily year-round.
Lunch: 11:30 a.m. - 3:30 p.m.
Dinner: 5-10 p.m. (Sunday to
Thursday), 5-11 p.m. (Friday and
Saturday).

Maison Earle is a lovely, two-storeyed inn furnished in early French-Canadian style. It was originally built as a private home for Robert Earle, a carriage maker in the early 1880s. The Earle family prospered and the house was used as a family home until it was sold after the death of Verva, the last descendant. Jean Boisvert, the inn manager, tells me that Verva has not really left the place. He reports various reminders of her presence, including that of a Christmas wreath which mysteriously flew off the fireplace and into the room of diners — exciting, but a little disconcerting nonetheless.

Bob Laflamme, our host, has a background typical of the area — French-Canadian father, Irish mother. The Irish came to this area in the early 19th Century to work the great forests of the Ottawa Valley, rafting their harvest down the Ottawa River to Montreal and Quebec. The French had settled the area a century before, wresting viable farms from the rock and bush of the Canadian Shield.

Situated in the Gatineau Hills just outside of Hull, the inn is a perfect meeting place for skiers and tourists. They can usually be found in the piano bar located on the second floor, lifting a cool one and relishing the delicious fried zucchini.

We were there for lunch. I enjoyed a delicious ham and melted cheese sandwich on homemade bread. My daughter, Joan, chose the house salad with garlic.

Bob tells me the favourites for dinner are Chateaubriand for two and Rack of Lamb, also for two. The regular menu features such delicacies as Steak Diane and Veal stuffed with ham and cheese and then sautéed. The fish menu is highlighted by poached salmon flavoured with hollandaise sauce. To finish off, you are invited to try their Irish or Spanish coffee or their very special Café Maison Earle. *Prices:* expensive.

Directions: Proceed north from Hull on Route 105, 40 kilometres (25 miles) to Wakefield.

Mooreside Tearoom and Museum

Barnes Rd.
Gatineau Park, Québec

Innkeeper: National Capital Commission
Telephone: 819-827-2020
Facilities: Tearoom. Open daily from Victoria Day until Thanksgiving, from late morning until early evening. Not licensed.

Mackenzie King was Prime Minister of Canada for 22 years, longer than any Prime Minister in the history of the British Commonwealth. His diaries reveal a lonely, eccentric person, but he has gone down in history as one of Canada's great Prime Ministers.

Mooreside Cottage became Mackenzie King's summer retreat almost from the moment he came to Ottawa at the turn of the century. As I wandered around the grounds of this magnificent estate in Kingsmere, I began to understand why it came to mean so much to him. Eventually it became a secluded hideaway where, through the years, he sank deeper into himself and his mysticism.

So important was Mooreside to King that he took steps to ensure that it would become one of Canada's national treasures. "I bequeath my Kingsmere properties to Canada as a thank-offering for the opportunity of public service which the people of my country have given me." Thus, this curious mixture of genuine architectural ruin and fabricated artifact set in the magnificent woodlands of the Gatineau Hills became a monument to Mackenzie King and the Canadian people as well.

The quaint Mooreside Cottage, which King originally obtained from the Herridge family at the turn of the century, was expanded by him through the years. Later, the National Capital Commission began a programme of restoration and rehabilitation both for the cottage and the ruins scattered around the estate.

A lovely way to visit Kingsmere is to drive up the Gatineau Parkway on a brilliant sunny morning in any season and spend a few hours wandering around the estate viewing the ruins. Sated with history and Canadiana, you can then retire to Mooreside for a delightful light lunch, selecting from a menu that includes salads, sandwich plates, quiches and the ever-present tourtière. You can finish off with some delightful scones, lemon loaf and home style apple pie with hot maple syrup. *Prices:* inexpensive.

Directions: From Hull, drive up the Gatineau Parkway a few miles to the Mackenzie King Estate and Mooreside.

Quebec City Region

Quebec was founded in 1608 and is the oldest walled city in North America. Entering the walled city through one of its three gates, one is transported into a 17th-Century city with narrow streets and the buildings crowding up to the street line. Today that charm is preserved and enhanced by a vigilant government ever watchful to preserve its heritage of historical buildings. For the history buff or simply the tourist in search of an unusual experience, the walled city of Quebec is certainly unique.

In the surrounding area, Île d'Orléans is a storehouse of history. One of the inns still boasts an outside wall pock-marked by shells from General Wolfe's invasion fleet of 1759.

The Quebec City area is the very heart of the Ancien Régime (the old era before 1760) and should not be missed on a visit to the province.

Quebec City Region

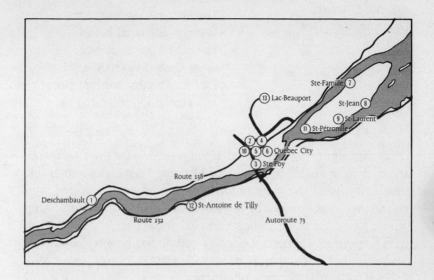

1   Auberge du Roy
2   Aux Anciens Canadiens
3   Château Bonne Entente
4   Château Frontenac
5   Hôtel Clarendon
6   La Crémaillère
7   L'Âtre
8   Le Domaine de Seigneur Mauvide
9   Le Moulin de St-Laurent
10 Maison d'Artigny
11 Manoir de l'Anse
12 Manoir de Tilly
13 Manoir St-Castin

Auberge du Roy

106, rue St-Laurent
Deschambault, Québec
G0A 1S0

Innkeepers: Yolande and Yvan Tremblay
Telephone: 418-286-6958
Rooms: 6 (4 shared baths)
Rates: (M.A.P.) moderate
Credit Cards: MasterCard, Visa
Facilities: Dining, outdoor pool and tennis. Open March to December.

Unfortunately for us, we visited L'Auberge du Roy prior to dinner and thus were unable to partake of Madame Tremblay's remarkable cuisine. It was all the more unfortunate because as we visited with Yolande we were seduced by the aroma of a delicious vegetable soup simmering on the stove. Delicate and indelicate hints about sampling went unnoticed. However Yolande's cuisine has been celebrated in Montreal's *Le Devoir* and even in the good gray Toronto *Globe and Mail*, self-styled Canada's national newspaper.

Zephrian Perrault designed this glorious "Little White Château" in 1860, and it remained a family residence until 1971 when the Tremblay family bought it. Mrs. Stewart, one of the more celebrated owners, was honoured, in 1919, by a visit from the Duke of Kent who shared a cup of tea with her.

The Tremblays are still considered newcomers by the villagers who refer to them as "Les Gens du Château" (The Château People). The cuisine provided by the whole family is renowned in the area as well as Quebec City and its environs.

Yvan makes daily trips to a nearby Quebec City market to find the makings for traditional Québécois dishes like frog's legs and scallops, as well as North American steaks, escalope of veal, filet of sole and Dover sole. *Prices:* moderate.

Directions: Deschambault is a few kilometres west of Quebec City, on Route 138.

Aux Anciens Canadiens

34, rue St-Louis
Québec, Québec
G1R 3Z1

Innkeeper: Mme Annette Légaré
Telephone: 418-692-1627
Credit Cards: All major cards
Facilities: Dining. Open daily year-round (11 a.m. - 10 p.m.). Fully licensed.

For many decades, this 17th-Century house was rumoured to be the place where General Montcalm died after being wounded in the Battle of the Plains of Abraham in 1759. However, recent historical research has shown that he actually died further down the road in the home of a Doctor Arnoux.

Wherever Montcalm may have expired, this building continued to play a significant part in the history of the city. It was the home of many notable people, including Philippe Aubert-de-Gaspé, author of the novel *Les Anciens Canadiens* from which the restaurant gets its name. It was also recently declared an historical site by the Quebec Government.

The architecture and construction is typical of the time with thick white-plastered walls, sturdy joists, and a steeply pitched Norman roof with dormer windows.

The menu is traditional Québécois fare and I was served a pâté of pork liver and a crock of pork and beans. A delicious bowl of zucchini soup was followed by the main course of potted beef and kidney pie "as Grand-mère would have made it". For dessert, I was served homemade yogurt with maple syrup.

Other favourites include L'assiette des habitants — a traditional Quebec country dish with tourtière, ragout, and crispy salt pork slices, lamb in blueberry wine sauce and duckling with maple syrup. *Prices:* expensive.

Château Bonne Entente

3400, Chemin Ste-Foy
Ste-Foy, Québec
G1X 1S6

Innkeepers: J.H. Mowbray Jones and Michel Bélanger
Telephone: 418-653-5221
Rooms: 102 (all with bath)
Rates: inexpensive-to-moderate
Credit Cards: All major cards
Facilities: Dining, outdoor pool, tennis, skating. Open year-round.

When one approaches Le Château Bonne Entente by way of the expansive estate, the impression one gets is that you are visiting a grand old seigneur from the 18th Century. In fact, the architecture is a faithful reproduction of a 19th-Century manor house.

Colonel Jones, as he was called, settled his family in Montreal and prospered there in the shipping business. In 1945, he bought this 120 acres of farmland to create a domain for a gentleman farmer and built his château on the foundations of a home occupied by the Shee family for over a hundred years.

Jones's ancestry goes back to Virginia Loyalists who came to Canada in 1775. His choice of the name Bonne Entente reflects his desire to improve the relationship between English and French. His dedication is evident in his traditional "Bonne Entente" greeting to his neighbours and guests.

Today, le Château operates as a modern inn under the ownership of the Jones family unit with Michel Bélanger as its chief executive officer. To help celebrate the coming of the Tall Ships to Quebec in 1984, Jones has had the family art collection, depicting sailing vessels, moved to the Château.

Château Bonne Entente is very comfortable and gracious. The front lawn is graced with a pond inhabited by a number of white geese. In the winter, it serves as a delightful skating rink. The original dining room and reading room, decorated in natural maple, are reminiscent of a more gracious and less hectic time.

The restaurant features French haute cuisine. The favourites are veal escalopes Marsala, pepper steak flambé and intriguing specialties, such as quail in wine and duckling in peach sauce. *Prices:* moderate-to-expensive.

Directions: Ste-Foy is just south of Quebec City. The Château is near the intersection of Autoroute Henri IV and Chemin Ste-Foy.

❧❧❧❧❧❧❧❧❧❧❧❧❧❧❧❧❧❧❧❧❧❧❧❧❧❧❧❧❧❧❧

Château Frontenac

1, rue des Carrières
Québec, Québec
G1R 4P5

Innkeeper: Canadian Pacific
Telephone: 418-692-3861
(1-800-268-9420)
Rooms: 523
Rates: moderate-to-expensive
Credit Cards: All major cards
Facilities: Dining, tobogganing, all summer and winter sports nearby.

I have been to Quebec many times and am always awed at how the Château dominates the walled city.

However, two incidents stand out in my mind. The first in 1969 when, as proud parents, we went to watch our son Larry play in the world famous Peewee Hockey Tournament. At that time we stayed at the Chateau with many of the other hockey parents. What excitement! Young boys and their families from all over Canada and the United States wandering through the lobbies; the colour and gaiety of Le Carnaval itself; and the fun of a toboggan ride down the Dufferin Terrace. The other time, just a few years ago, I was in Quebec over Easter and enjoyed La Fête de Pâques brunch there. As I was showing off my strangulated French, the waiter, with a bored look, said, "I can't understand your French. Please speak English." That certainly put me in my place.

Le Château Frontenac was built in 1893 on the site of the old Château St-Louis, residence of the governors of New France. The current Château bears little resemblance to the former structure. Where the present-day Château is the essence of luxury and comfort, the Château St-Louis was constantly in need of repair. The governors' pleas for funds for repairs fell on deaf ears back in France.

With the addition of various wings from 1899 to 1924, the Château has grown both in size and stature. In 1943, it was the sight of a war conference held by Churchill, Roosevelt and Mackenzie King. Other

world leaders, including General de Gaulle of France and Madame Chiang-Kai-shek, have been guests at the Château.

There are many fine inns in the Quebec City area, but no trip to the city would be complete without a visit to this grand and historic hotel.

Hôtel Clarendon

57, rue Ste-Anne
Québec, Québec
G1R 3X4

Innkeeper: Jacques Cyr
Telephone: 418-692-2480
Rooms: 99, with bath
Rates: moderate
Credit Cards: All major cards
Facilities: Dining

The Clarendon is right in the heart of the old city of Quebec and is a perfect introduction to it. This unique hotel was the meeting place for the Quebec bourgeoisie in the early years of the century and remains today an important cultural landmark.

The hotel was originally the site of a house built at least 200 years ago. In 1790, it became Quebec's first theatre, The Hay Market Theatre. In 1817, it became the hotel that is now recognized as Quebec's oldest. It has recently been renovated to highlight its Art Nouveau architecture. The main dining room has been named after Charles Baillairgé, the Quebec architect, to commemorate his contribution to the culture of the province.

The chef at the Clarendon is Hervé Labarre, arguably the best chef in the area. He prepares a meal with the quality and attention of a small restaurant.

La Crémaillère

21, rue St-Stanislas
Québec, Québec
G1R 1S4

Innkeeper: Peppino Boezio
Telephone: 418-692-2216
Credit Cards: All major cards
Facilities: Dining. Fully licensed.
Open daily year-round. Lunch:
11:30 a.m. - 2:30 p.m. (Monday to
Friday), Dinner: 5:30-11 p.m.
(Monday to Sunday).

In 1764, the British General James Murray built a home on this site that remained in the family until 1801. Later, the building we now see was built by Louis Latouche, a master mason, for his use as a home. It is a five-storeyed building of stone, similar to many of the buildings on the narrow streets of the old walled city. At the time the building was designated a historical site, the owner was a Mr. Adams.

The main floor is now a very fine restaurant under the direction of Peppino Boezio. The menu features a mixture of pastas and veals reflecting Peppino's Italian origins (he came to Quebec from Italy in 1969). One can enjoy fettucini, lasagna and spaghetti of various kinds, as well as veal scallopini. The traditional Quebec rack of lamb, frog's legs, shrimps, scallops and scampi complete the menu.

Accompanied by Quebec Tourism representative Jacques Auclair and his charming wife Louiselle, I enjoyed the Fettucini Crémaillère. The total price for three meals, including two bottles of wine and tip, was $87.00. *Prices:* expensive.

⚜⚜⚜⚜⚜⚜⚜⚜⚜⚜⚜⚜⚜⚜⚜⚜⚜⚜⚜⚜⚜⚜⚜⚜⚜

L'Âtre

4403, Chemin Royal
Ste-Famille, Île d'Orléans
Québec G0A 3P0

Innkeeper: Suzanne H. Demers
Telephone: 418-829-2474
Credit Cards: MasterCard, Visa, American Express
Facilities: Dining. Fully licensed.
Open May to October (noon to 10 p.m.)

It's rather difficult to know where to start in describing L'Âtre. After parking in a lot nearby, an ancient calèche with a coachman in period costume takes you to the restaurant. There, you will meet Suzanne, the proprietor of this fantastic inn. A writer of extreme sensitivity, she has prepared a pamphlet, A *Plea for a House of Stone*, in which she recounts the sense of rejuvenation she feels when returning to l'Âtre each spring. The menu's introduction is a poem composed by Suzanne whose last lines express, better than anything, her feelings about L'Âtre.

> More possessed than a possessor
> I dare not alter its appearance
> For fear of spoiling its beauty
> Too fragile to stand my tampering.

This ancestral home of the Gagnon family was built in 1680 and has been classified by the Quebec Government as an historic building. The fieldstone building has walls over three feet thick and an uneven, rough-hewn pine floor. While waiting for dinner, guests may go upstairs to the attic to enjoy a drink and play a few board games.

In the candle-lit dining room, Suzanne prepares her favourites from the menu. They are the traditional Québécois foods — a terrine of rabbit in cognac, roast pheasant in mint sauce, and a family recipe of Royale Régal du Diable la Tourtière (tourtière with devil's relish). *Prices:* moderate.

Suzanne was most enthusiastic about another traditional Quebec dessert called Tartine d'Antan (of days gone by) made up of bread, maple sugar and fresh homemade cream.

If you come on the right evening you may be entertained by local musicians who are in concert three times per week. Prepare for an exciting adventure in history, food, music and, above all, the lively hospitality of Suzanne, an unusual woman of many talents.

Directions: Île d'Orléans is across the river by bridge from Quebec City.

Le Domaine de Seigneur Mauvide

1451, avenue Royale
St-Jean, Île d'Orléans
Québec G0A 3W0

Innkeeper: Antoine Pouliot
Telephone: 418-829-2915
Credit Cards: MasterCard, Visa,
American Express
Facilities: Dining. Fully licensed.
Open daily: 11:30 a.m. - 10 p.m.
(mid-June to September). Sunday
Brunch: October to May

According to a research paper written by Denis Tétrault in 1981, le Domaine was originally built by Jean Mauvide in 1734, and added to as his needs and wealth increased. He goes on to say that the manor house is the most important lay building constructed under the French to come down to us in its original state. This original state includes marks left on walls by cannonballs during British Admiral Saunders' invasion in 1759. His fleet landed on Île d'Orléans to prepare their assault on Quebec. He also says that it is a good example of French architecture adapted to the climate and the materials available in New France.

After 1734, Mauvide, a Royal surgeon, added to his property until it became a seigneury in 1752.

Tétrault also indicates in his research just how much wealth

Mauvide amassed as a seigneur, and found that the property remained in the family until 1927 when it was sold to Judge J. Camille Pouliot, grandfather of the present owner. It is now designated as an historical site by the Quebec Government and has become a restaurant-museum.

Because this establishment has such a rich historical background, it is only proper that the menu reflect its French origins, but updated by modern Québécois cuisine. As Antoine indicated to me, the favourite items on the menu are the seafood casserole with scallops, shrimps, mussels, salmon and crab in a white lobster sauce topped with Gruyère cheese. There is also a game specialty for two, maître-chasseur, which is half a pheasant, a partridge, and two quails with fresh vegetables. *Prices:* moderate.

Directions: Île d'Orléans is across the river by bridge from Quebec City.

❧❧❧❧❧❧❧❧❧❧❧❧❧❧❧❧❧❧❧❧❧❧❧❧❧

Le Moulin de Saint-Laurent

754, avenue Royale, C.P. 72
St-Laurent, Île d'Orléans
Québec J0A 3Z0

Innkeepers: Amee Van Veen and André Tanguay
Telephone: 418-829-3888
Credit Cards: MasterCard, Visa, American Express
Facilities: Dining. Fully licensed. Open daily May to October, 10 a.m. to 10 p.m.

Le Moulin de Saint-Laurent, located on the south shore of Île d'Orléans, was originally known as Le Moulin du Sud when it was first built in 1635. For over 250 years, it produced the flour for villagers living on the island's south shore. Every night the mill wheel was brought indoors to protect it from the weather. Aside from the mill artifacts which can be seen everywhere, the porch remains as a charming reminder of the mill's past, overlooking the millrun and providing pleasant summer dining.

An inn cannot be considered genuine unless it has a ghost and Amee did not hesitate in telling me about theirs. According to traditional island myth, the chairs and tables in the mill kept flying around for no apparent reason. A priest was called in to exorcise the ghost.

Apparently, he displeased the ghost and died in the process. Later, an older and more experienced priest was brought in and he successfully exorcised the nasty old ghost.

In 1963, John Van Veen bought the mill and turned it into a very successful restaurant providing evening entertainment in the form of concerts. Recently, Amee decided to carry on the family tradition and is operating the restaurant, while her father still provides some of the music.

We had a delicious lunch. Cream of mushroom soup followed by Sandwich Annette with ham, tomato, egg and lettuce. Lionel Poulin, my companion from the Ministry of Industry, Trade and Tourism, enjoyed a special French-Canadian style pâté with green pepper. The dining menu sparkles with dishes Amee's mother brought from Holland, such as Smoked eel Dutch style and Neptune veal cutlet. Other items include snails with pernod on pastry shells and a centre of Filet Mignon with mushrooms. *Prices:* moderate-to-expensive.

Directions: Île d'Orléans is across the river by bridge from Quebec City.

Maison d'Artigny
(Le Keg and Brandy's)
690-4 Grande-Allée
Québec, Québec
G1R 2K4

Innkeeper: Jacques Michaud
Telephone: 418-529-0068
Credit Cards: All major cards
Facilities: Dining. Fully licensed.
Open daily, noon until closing.

Both the Maison d'Artigny and the building next door, La Brasserie Grande-Allée, have been designated by the Ministry of Culture as historical sites. The Brasserie was built in the late 18th Century by Gérald Houde and at one time served as a bank. Its vault continues to preserve things precious, as it now functions as a giant beer cooler.

Because of its historical designation, Jacques has gone through all sorts of negotiations with the authorities over the matter of the design of a sign which would involve the removal of the old Maison d'Artigny name from the face of the building. This is an indication of how important historical preservation is to the Québécois.

The restaurant is part of the The Keg franchise which specializes in steaks and seafood. I enjoyed a deliciously prepared steak. The menu featured other delicacies such as scallops en brochette, snow crabs, shrimps and seafood platter. Of course, there was a generous and interesting salad bar included in the meal. *Prices:* moderate.

❖❖❖❖❖❖❖❖❖❖❖❖❖❖❖❖❖❖❖❖❖❖❖❖❖

Manoir de l'Anse
22, avenue du Quai
Ste-Pétronille, Île d'Orléans
Québec G0A 4C0

Innkeeper: Claude Gauthier
Telephone: 418-828-2248
Rooms: 34 (18 with bath)
Rates: very inexpensive
Credit Cards: MasterCard, Visa,
American Express
Facilities: Dining, outdoor pool,
river swimming, snowshoeing,
cross-country skiing.

My company on this tour of Île d'Orléans was Lionel Poulin of the Quebec Ministry of Industry, Trade and Tourism who have been extremely helpful throughout. After a few minutes it appeared that we had passed by the Manoir. It was then that Lionel, with a sheepish little smile, told me that in its earlier days the Manoir was known as

Maison de la Débaucherie — and he was reluctant to admit that he knew where it was. You can bet that I spent the rest of the day reminding him about that.

The Manoir was built as an inn in 1900, catering mostly to wealthy American tourists who came for the summer with their families. The original *aubergiste* was the owner of a New York shipping company who would arrive by boat from New York.

In celebration of Jacques Cartier's discovery of Canada in 1534, the Tall Ships of the world sailed down the St. Lawrence and docked, for a week in June of 1984, right beside the Manoir. Guests were able to view this magnificent sight from the porch and from the new patio that Claude had built to overlook the river.

The Manoir has a mixture of French and Victorian architecture. The turrets and dormer windows are typically French; but the simple rectangular lay-out of the building, with its enclosed porches, reminds me of an old Victorian summer home.

The table d'hôte menu features Escalope of veal, a fondue Chinoise and Chateaubriand (for two). Other items include pepper steak, filet of sole and scallops in a pastry shell. *Prices:* moderate.

Directions: Île d'Orléans is across the river by bridge from Quebec City.

Manoir de Tilly

3854, Chemin de Tilly
St-Antoine-de-Tilly, Québec
G0S 2C0

Innkeepers: Jocelyne and Majella Gagnon
Telephone: 418-477-2407
Rooms: 6 (1 with bath)
Rates: very inexpensive
Credit Cards: MasterCard, Visa, American Express
Facilities: Dining, outdoor pool.
Open May 1 to October 15.

Manoir de Tilly, built as a seigneurial mansion almost 200 years ago, has (for the past 65 years) been an inn. We were quaffing a beer on the patio out back overlooking the vegetable garden and the Saint Lawrence when Jocelyne told us a story about some recent history of the inn. Apparently some gentleman from Quebec City used to rent the whole place for a weekend to play poker and to do other things. Common sense and a good sense of propriety prevented me from asking what those "other things" were.

The Manoir was founded in 1786 by Jean-Baptiste Noël, who was Seigneur de Tilly, Bonsécours et Maranda as well as Captain of the Military. It remained the seigneury residence through four generations of the Noël family until 1893.

Around the end of the First World War, the manoir became an inn along with a century-old schoolhouse which now accommodates three rooms on its second floor. All rooms in both buildings are individually and charmingly decorated.

Jocelyne maintains a vegetable garden off the patio behind the manoir where she has been known to recount stories of the manoir's history and its sometimes eccentric guests. Her fresh vegetables grace the dining table in such dishes as the Soupe à la Gourgane. House specialties include Beef Bourgignon, Coq-au-vin and Tourtière Saguenienne (Saguenay), a traditional recipe with beef, pork and wild rabbit.

One of the desserts, Trempettes à la crème et sucre du pays, is simply fresh bread soaked in homemade cream and maple sugar. Somewhat heavy on the calories I would think, but apparently delicious.

Directions: St-Antoine-de-Tilly is on the south shore Route 132, a few kilometres west of Quebec City.

Manoir St-Castin

99, Chemin le Tour du Lac
Lac-Beauport, Québec
G0A 2C0

Innkeepers: Guy Beaurivage and Louis Maurice Wong Kee Song
Telephone: 418-849-4461 (1-800-268-9051)
Rooms: 48 (all with bath)
Rates: expensive-to-moderate
Credit Cards: All major cards
Facilities: Dining. Alpine and cross-country skiing, lake and pool swimming, tennis, boating. Open year-round.

Louis Maurice very kindly gave me a copy of André Duval's *Lac Beauport, Mon Lac ce Raconte*, which was produced in 1973 in cooperation with the Municipal Council of Lac-Beauport. It traces the history of the region to its first seigneurs, Giffard and Duschenay, during the founding of Quebec City in the early 17th Century. The book quotes George Gail in *Historic Tales of Old Quebec*: "The Lake for years was the most popular resort in the vicinity of the city, not alone for civilians, but for officers of the Imperial Army . . . garrisoned at the Citadel. . . . While on their fishing excursions, they were usually the guests of the Pépins, whose hotel, now known as Bagouettes, occupied such a commanding position at the lakeside."

Thus, the current Manoir St-Castin began as a hotel as far back as 1850. Today, it ranks as one of the premier summer and winter resorts on the continent and has survived three disastrous fires, the last one in 1959. Now the manoir is an ultra-modern and beautifully appointed inn on breathtaking Lac-Beauport, offering superb ambience both to the vacationer and to the daytripper from the Quebec City area.

Chef André Morizot, from France's wine country, has created a cuisine that ranks with the best in Quebec. The menu describes, with loving detail, such delicacies as oven-roasted pheasant deliciously served in a rich brown porto and blueberry sauce. Other specialties are Filet Mignon stuffed with duck liver, medallions of lamb browned in butter and filet of sole stuffed with duck liver, medallions of lamb browned in butter and filet of sole stuffed with mussels, cod, liver, shrimps and mushrooms. *Prices:* expensive.

Directions: Lac-Beauport can be reached from Quebec City on Autoroute 73 to Exit #157. Follow the signs to Lac-Beauport.

Montreal Area and the Laurentians

Because of its strategic position dominating the travel routes to and from the interior of North America, Montreal has been and still is a major world port. Named after its famous Mount Royal, it is a city with lots of "pizazz" — a fascinating combination of the Old World and the New and of French and English. Its people from many lands give the city a truly cosmopolitan gaiety.

The Laurentians were originally developed as a colonization area to encourage late 19th-Century French Canadians to settle there rather than leave the province for other parts of North America. This experiment was mostly a failure, but it left a network of roads and railways which opened the way for timber and, later, tourist development.

On the south shore, in the Richelieu Valley, the traveller finds one of the oldest settled areas in Quebec. It has been rich farmland for over 300 years. In this area also were fought the battles of the Rebellion of 1837-38. A visit to the local librarian will put you in touch with all the landmarks of the Rebellion as well as bring you up to date on the significant events surrounding it.

Montreal Area and the Laurentians

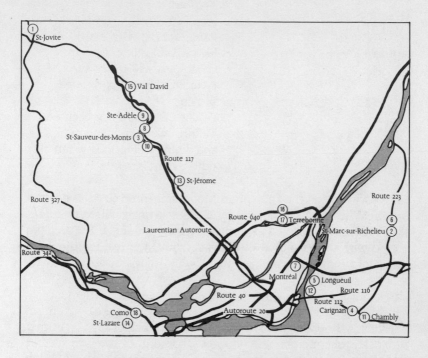

1   Auberge Gray Rocks Inn
2   Auberge Handfield
3   Auberge St-Denis
4   Au Tournant de la Rivière
5   Au Vieux Longueuil
6   Hostellerie Les Trois Tilleuls
7   Hôtel Ritz-Carlton
8   La Maison Victorienne
9   L'Auberge de Nice

10   La Vieille Ferme de 1900
11   Le Bistro Illico
12   Le Relais Terrapin
13   Le Vieux Moulin
14   Mon Village
15   Parker's Lodge
16   Restaurant à l'Étang des Moulins
17   Restaurant Phidimus
18   Willow Inn

Auberge Gray Rocks Inn

PO Box 1000
St-Jovite, Québec
J0T 2H0

Innkeeper: Biff Wheeler
Telephone: 819-425-2771
(or 1-800-567-6767)
Rooms: 252 (all with bath)
Rates: (A.P.) moderate
Credit Cards: All major cards,
including Diners' and Carte
Blanche
Facilities: Dining. Fully licensed.
Tennis, water sports, downhill
and alpine skiing, riding and all
other resort features.

Gray Rocks Inn, in the Laurentian Mountains some 90 miles north of Montreal, was the site chosen by George Wheeler of New York in 1896, for the building of a sawmill and lumber business. The area prospered with the extension of railways from Montreal to St-Jovite in 1903. Unfortunately, a raging forest fire in 1905 put an end to the thriving endeavour.

However, the rail link established to facilitate settlement and development brought a new kind of business to the area — tourism. The next year, George and his wife, Lucille, began to take in their American fishermen buddies as guests, sometimes flying them in to fish Lac-Ouimet or to play the first Laurentians golf course, established in 1922.

In the 1930s, development of the ski slopes began and with a series of internationally famous ski instructors, a world-class family ski centre was established — the Snow Eagle Ski School. Ninety percent of the slopes have snow-making equipment and guests can enjoy skiing from late November till May.

One of the products of the ski development was the emergence of their own family world-ski champion Lucile, granddaughter of the founder. She won many gold medals in European and North American championships in the 1940s and 1950s, along with other Gray Rocks stalwarts, such as the Wurtelle twins and Jack "Porky" Griffin.

To accommodate the fast-growing tennis craze of the mid-1970s and to honour their tradition of providing excellence of training in both skiing and tennis, the famous Dennis Van der Meer Tennis University was established with 14 Har-Tru courts.

The inn itself is a multi-turreted building in the grand Victorian manner. Recently, the Wheeler family purchased an existing lodge nearby and turned it into the luxurious Le Château with its own dining lounge and heated swimming pool.

So celebrated is Gray Rocks Inn that it was awarded the Mobil Travel Guide *Four-Star Award* for excellence in both the facilities and its continental cuisine — a tribute to the generations of Wheelers who have extended the Laurentian hospitality down through the years.

Directions: Follow the Laurentian Autoroute north 134 kilometres (83 miles) to Ste-Agathe and beyond to Route 117 and St-Jovite and then Highway 327 north to Gray Rocks.

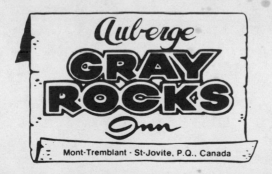

Auberge GRAY ROCKS Inn
Mont-Tremblant · St-Jovite, P.Q., Canada

Auberge Handfield

555, boulevard Richelieu
St-Marc-sur-Richelieu, Québec
JoL 2Eo

Innkeeper: Conrad Handfield
Telephone: 514-584-2226
Rooms: 38, all with bath
Rates: inexpensive
Facilities: Dining, swimming pool, marina, cross-country skiing. Fully licensed.

When I was talking to the francophone but bilingual Conrad Handfield, I mentioned that his name sounded English. "My ancestors were part of Wolfe's invading army in 1759," was his answer. The next day I crossed the Richelieu River on a little 3-car ferry at St-Charles. As the ferry approached, I noticed it carried two flags — one of the flags, the flag of the Patriotes (those who rebelled in 1837-8) flying above the Maple Leaf. I was slightly unsettled by this and asked the captain about it. "Oh, it's just a tourist gimmick."

Thus, in a period of twenty-four hours, I was forcibly reminded of the sharp ebb and flow of Quebec history. The successful invasion of the English in 1759 was, in 1837, partially responsible for the rebellion led by the Patriotes in the Richelieu area.

The Auberge Handfield belonged to Conrad's grandmother, and his entire family has been involved in building up the property to reflect the 150-year-old history of the area.

The Auberge consists of a main house and seven cottages that

have been carefully moved from their original location in the surrounding area and relocated on Handfield property. Conrad and his family have gone to great pains to gather genuine antique Quebec furniture to furnish the rooms, and even located a grandfather clock with a wooden mechanism. A few miles away, he maintains a 19th-Century maple sugar shack and, in March and April, he hosts sugaring off parties for his guests and friends.

Conrad also purchased an old ferry boat and refurnished it as a summer theatre/restaurant. L'Escale's professional acting company performs from mid-June to the end of August.

Madame Handfield specializes and expands on old French-Canadian recipes developed by Conrad's mother when the Auberge first opened as a restaurant in the 1940s. Specialties, such as tourtière, rabbit, sugar pie and roast duck, are staples of the menu. The Galettes de Sarrasin — buckwheat cakes with delicious, thick local maple syrup, were my choice for breakfast.

The menu also features a Nouvelle Cuisine Française with such delicacies as potted minced goose in white wine, a terrine of salmon mousse with cucumber sauce, escalope of veal bergère and Filet Mignon Forestière.

Directions: Proceed east from Montreal on Autoroute 20 a few miles to Exit #112. Take Route 223, 8 kilometres (5 miles) north to St-Marc.

Auberge St-Denis

61, rue St-Denis
St-Sauveur-des-Monts, Québec
J0R 1R0

Innkeeper: Richard Desjardins
Telephone: 514-227-4766
Rooms: 10 (5 with bath)
Rates: very inexpensive
Credit Cards: All major cards
Facilities: Dining. Swimming pool.
Golf, tennis, skiing, sailing
packages arranged. Open year-round. Fully licensed.

I walked into the Auberge St-Denis and was met by Richard Desjardins, the innkeeper. With his handlebar moustache and sweater thrown casually over his shoulders, he looked like a young World-War-II air force officer on leave. Given the history of the inn, it could be said that Richard had taken on some of the character of its past.

Originally known as The Old Country Inn, it was built around 1940 to house some eighty children of aristocratic British families who had been sent to safety in Canada during the bombing of Britain. In order for the children to continue their education, the province designated the Inn as a school until the end of the war, when most of the children returned to their families in England.

Richard and his family, on visiting St-Sauveur, were immediately struck by the possibilities for The Old Country Inn, now almost completely abandoned and run down. Thus, in 1979, the Desjardins family bought the inn and completely remodelled it, retaining its gracious country look and adding a patio and swimming pool.

The two-storeyed inn has two dining rooms on the main floor and eleven rooms on the second floor. They are simple but comfortable rooms with a wonderful view of the Laurentians.

Richard and his family have always offered a warm welcome to their visitors, whether they come for his famous Sunday Brunch or to stay for a few days. Summer and winter, Richard takes advantage of the inn's proximity to the mountains by making special arrangements for his guests to enjoy the great recreational facilities of the area, be it reduced ski-lift rates, horseback riding, sailing, golf or tennis. Of course, just a walk or drive through the mountains is sufficient vacation for many.

I arrived for lunch and was able to sit out on the patio. The brunch was colourfully spread out and included fresh vegetables, sausages, tourtière and meats. The dinner menu features pheasant, duck and partridge. For those whose tastes are not so gamey, Richard serves sweetbreads in Côte d'Azur sauce, Lobster Thermidor, Scallops of salmon in Grenbloise sauce and seafood crêpes. His mother is particularly proud of her rum pie dessert as well as the Chef fraiserie (strawberry cake). *Prices:* moderate.

While sitting over dinner, I was transported back to the 1940s of The Old Country Inn by the "big band" sound of Glenn Miller and Tommy Dorsey in the background. Richard tells me that he makes a point of playing this kind of music as a tribute to the era of the Inn's founding and for the enjoyment of his guests. During the Sunday evening meal hour, such artists as guitarist Marcel Gervais and violoncellist Claude Ferland entertain.

Directions: Leave the Laurentian Autoroute from Montreal at Exit #58 for St-Sauveur.

❧❧❧❧❧❧❧❧❧❧❧❧❧❧❧❧❧❧❧❧❧❧❧❧❧❧❧❧❧❧

Au Tournant de la Rivière

5070, rue Salaberry
Carignan, Québec
J3L 3P9

Innkeeper: Jacques Robert
Telephone: 514-658-7372
Credit Cards: Visa, American Express, Carte Blanche
Facilities: Dining. Fully licensed. Open year-round, Tuesday to Saturday. Dinner: 6:30—9:30 p.m.

Just a few miles east of Montreal, housed in an historic barn, Au Tournant de la Rivière is a mecca for serious diners. In October 1981, the *Montreal Calendar* wrote that Jacques was the new leader of a Montreal cuisine. Guests can watch as Jacques cooks their meals lightly and quickly just before serving. Devoted to his craft, Jacques even spends his nights off cooking and entertaining friends.

Built by the Bisaillons, this turn-of-the-century barn remained in the family until its purchase by Jacques, who proceeded to renovate extensively. A glassed-in patio was being prepared during my visit to provide additional summer and winter dining. The interior is decorated with various pieces of work by local artisans. The ceiling is supported by actual tree trunks, bark and all, and bales of treated hay can still be found in the hayloft, all of which add to the rustic charm of the restaurant.

The cuisine, however, is what has attracted guests. Most popular with diners is the Dégustation pour Tous — a six-course meal priced at $40.00, but well worth it. Other menu items include: Noisettes d'agneaux echalotes (filet of lamb with onions); Aiguillettes de canard et sa cuisse confite (breast of duck with boiled red berries and ginger with the leg cooked slowly in the grease of the duck); and Blanc de pintade à la Crème Laitive et sa cuisse grillée (breast of guinea hen in cream, leg grilled). *Prices:* expensive.

Directions: Take Route 116 from Montreal to Route 112; proceed south a few kilometres to Carignan.

Au Vieux Longueuil

43 ouest, rue St-Charles
Longueuil, Québec

Innkeeper: André Lussier
Telephone: 514-670-8950
Credit Cards: All major cards
Facilities: Dining. Open daily for lunch and dinner.

Charles LeMoyne, the seigneur and founder of Longueuil, erected an immense fort on this site between 1685 and 1690. Approximately 64 metres by 52 metres, it was built completely of stone with four turrets for defence. It had barracks, cattle barns, a beautiful church, and stood on seigneurial land that stretched far from the St. Lawrence. It was also occupied by the invading American armies who were pushing towards Montreal in 1775.

In 1973, archeological work was done on the site. In the basement of the restaurant the remains of one of the walls of the fort was discovered. Because the fort had been completely demolished in 1810, this find was of great significance.

It is of more than passing interest to know that André Lussier himself arranged for the historical and archeological research. This is a testament to the extreme interest that many Québécois have in their history.

Today it is one of the most popular restaurants in Longueuil. André put me under the care of Lorette Laporte, a charming waitress who has been with the restaurant for ten years. For lunch she suggested the small steak with onions and mushrooms and a purée of vegetables and potatoes.

Lorette tells me the favourites for dinner are duck à l'orange, pork medallions with dried plum sauce and rack of lamb. Another specialty is usually found in the Quebec countryside under many names. Here it is called Country Style Maple Sugar Délice and consists of French bread with a double portion of fresh cream and maple sugar. *Prices:* moderate.

Directions: Longueuil is on the south shore of the St. Lawrence just opposite downtown Montreal.

Hostellerie Les Trois Tilleuls

290, rue Richelieu
St-Marc-sur-Richelieu, Québec
JoL 2E0

Innkeepers: Bernard Môme, Michel Aubriot, Michel Régnier
Telephone: 514-584-2231
Rooms: 21
Rates: moderate
Credit Cards: All major cards
Facilities: Dining, tennis, boating, marina, putting green, golf, and skiing nearby.

Les Trois Tilleuls is one of only four Canadian hostelries mentioned in the prestigious *Relais et Châteaux de France.* Not a castle nor a Swiss spa, this handsomely restored and refurbished farmhouse still stands proudly, on the shore of the historic and beautiful Richelieu River, ready to receive its many guests.

Jean-Paul Vary built this farmhouse in 1880 and prospered here. Many of his descendants still live in the area.

Nearby is an island which once was the site of a seminary since burned down. I was told that the name of the island was L'Île aux Cerfs, which means Deer Island. However, with a wink, I was given the explanation that the only "deers" that one hears of now on the island are terms of endearment for the lovers who sometimes frequent it.

Established in 1975 as a restaurant, Les Trois Tilleuls quickly grew into the renowned inn of today, with the addition of 21 rooms in 1981. Michel and his partners scoured the countryside for artifacts that would retain the rural Quebec ambience. The most striking of

these is a hay-drying piece that has been converted into a very attractive chandelier. Some furniture pieces are specially designed by area craftsmen.

Outside is a patio and a gazebo complete with an old-fashioned wooden swing.

Bernard suggests that the favourite items of the menu are escalope of salmon with sauce Smitaine, le Doré Trois Tilleuls, sweetbreads in white wine, and, finally, Chateaubriand with Bordelaise sauce. *Prices:* expensive.

Bernard's favourite dessert is La Marquise au chocolat served with a coffee sauce.

Directions: Take Autoroute 20 east out of Montreal to Exit #112. Go north on Route 223 a few kilometres to St-Marc.

❧❧❧❧❧❧❧❧❧❧❧❧❧❧❧❧❧❧❧❧❧❧

Hôtel Ritz-Carlton
1228 ouest, rue Sherbrooke
Montréal, Québec
H3G 1H6

Innkeeper: Intercontinental Hotels Ltd.
Telephone: 514-842-4212
Rooms: 247 (all with private baths)
Rates: expensive
Facilities: Dining

The Ritz-Carlton opened its doors on New Year's Eve, 1913. It was allowed to use the name "Ritz" because César Ritz of the famed Paris Ritz was satisfied that the Montreal hotel would reflect the same high quality of service and facilities. Today, so successfully has the Ritz maintained its standards that the American Automobile Association has given it the coveted *Five Diamond Award* "for excellence". It has been able to provide royal service while maintaining a friendly, caring concern for its guests. We even found the night elevator operator acting as baby-sitter, or dog-walker and general confidant. One has only to enter the intimate black and gold lobby or stay in the gracious high-ceilinged rooms to agree with one critic who called it "a bastion of elegance, refinement and sensibility."

From the outset, the guest list read like a cross between *Burke's Peerage* and the *International Who's Who,* as the Ritz became the watering place for the finest of Montreal's English community. People such as Sir Frederick William Taylor, President of the Bank of Montreal, and

Sir Montagu Allen, the shipping magnate, were frequent guests. Hugh McKay, a director of both Canadian Breweries and Montreal Light, Heat and Power used the Ritz as a permanent home, as did many others. Today, the Ritz attracts the "new royalty". Elizabeth Taylor and Richard Burton chose it as the site for their marriage in 1964, and the Rolling Stones visit the hotel whenever they are in Montreal.

The Ritz now serves as a meeting place for all members of the Montreal community. While strolling through its busy lobby I could overhear more than one international language, a feature characteristic of the city.

There are several bars and dining rooms to suit your taste and pocketbook. Downstairs is the casual L'Intercontinental for casual dining where I ate breakfasts during my stay. Also in the lower lobby is the famous Maritime Bar specializing in sea foods. Nearby is the Grand Prix, an elegant piano bar serving light meals late at night. I wandered into the Grand Prix after an exhausting train trip, and snacked on their delicious steak sandwich and beer. The weather did not permit me to visit the Ritz Garden situated in the hotel court-yard. I'm told it is a delightful feature not to be missed. However, we were fortunate to dine in the elegant Café de Paris. After a cocktail in the smart, stylish bar we moved into the very formal dining room.

Dinner here is an experience one must have at least once while staying at the Ritz. It is service and food deluxe. Appetizers include a choice of hors d'oeuvres, Prosciutto with tropical fruits or Mousseline of pike and salmon. A plate of crisp, fresh carrots, celery and, my passion, black olives is complimentary. The main course is brought to the table on a cart where final preparations are made. My friend ordered Veal Filet in white martini sauce nicely set off against a colourful selection of vegetables, such as carrots, potatoes and cauliflower. My choice was Rack of lamb, sliced at the table, with Dijon sauce, delicious and satisfying. Also available on the extensive menu are Scampis au Pernod, Grilled lamb chops, sauce Paloise and Feuilleté of fresh salmon à la Ritz.

Desserts are presented either on a wagon (fresh pineapple, strawberries, Kiwi pie) or to your order (Pears flambés with Pernod — $14.00 for two, Cherries Jubilee — $12.50 for two) both prepared at your table. *Prices:* expensive.

We finished off with fruits, cheese and coffee. The cost was a surprisingly low $46.00, including tip.

✤✤✤✤✤✤✤✤✤✤✤✤✤✤✤✤✤✤✤✤✤✤✤

La Maison Victorienne

231, rue Principale
St-Sauveur-des-Monts, Québec
J0R 1R0

Innkeeper: Peter Wenger
Telephone: 514-227-4585
Credit Cards: MasterCard, Visa, American Express
Facilities: Dining. Fully licensed. Open daily year-round: winter (4-11 p.m.), summer (3-11 p.m.) with Sunday brunch (noon-3 p.m.)

Right on the corner opposite the church on St-Sauveur's main street stands that town's other landmark — La Grosse Maison Bleue (The Big Blue House) known as La Maison Victorienne.

This house was originally built on property acquired by François-Xavier Clouthier in 1892. Marguerite Chevalier-Landreman, his 82-year-old daughter, remembers that he chose the model for his home from an American catalogue. Clouthier owned a general store, but prospered as a moneylender. Elected mayor in 1885, he held that position for 36 years, the longest of any mayor in the village.

Though St-Sauveur was founded in the 19th Century, it did not really come into its own until the 1920s and 1930s when downhill skiing became popular and people discovered this charming village nestled at the base of the Laurentians.

Credit for preserving the original Victorian grandeur of the home must go to Madame Trudolf who occupied the house from 1971. She engaged workers to restore the house while maintaining its usefulness.

La Maison Victorienne actually houses two restaurants. Le Bistro à Raclette serves five different fondues and a light menu. Le Restaurant l'Entrecôte has an à la carte and table d'hôte menu featuring Frog's Legs Provençale, Scampis in garlic butter and Beef. They also serve Medallions of veal in a cream sauce made with Port wine and sirloin steak with a choice of various sauces. *Prices:* moderate.

Directions: St-Sauveur can be reached at Exit #60 on the Laurentian Autoroute, approximately 50 kilometres (31 miles) north of Montreal.

L'Auberge de Nice

4196, boulevard Ste-Adèle
Ste-Adèle, Québec
JoR 1Lo

Innkeeper: Édouard Eysseric
Telephone: 514-227-2730
Credit Cards: MasterCard, Visa,
American Express, Enroute
Facilities: Dining. Fully licensed.
Open every day year-round from
6 p.m.

A few miles north of Ste-Adèle on Route 117 stands an unpretentious little log cabin, l'Auberge de Nice. However, do not be fooled by the simple, white-washed exterior or the quietly furnished interior. L'Auberge de Nice is aptly named after the Provençal origins of its owner and chef, Édouard Eysseric who in 1968 emigrated to Canada. He has brought his chef's background from France to this little outpost in Quebec's Laurentians. The summer cottagers and skiers from Montreal and as far away as Toronto have sought out this excellent little restaurant.

The buildings housing this restaurant were built 180 years ago. Originally it was two small log cabins — one from Mount Savage and the other from Lac-Miliette. I must say it was rather an odd way to enlarge one's home. Yet it remained a residence for Raymond Staub (who was born there) until he sold it to Édouard in 1976.

Since then it has been the happy fount of Provençale cuisine for the Laurentian area. Starting with its extensive wine list, mostly Provençale and Bourdelaise, we proceed to the special Provençal soup, soupe de poisson or the special soup of the house, vegetable soup with basil. The entrées include such delicacies as Civet de Lapin (rabbit stew), fresh Dover sole imported daily and Canard d'orange with Bigarade sauce. As an indication of the care Édouard takes in his meal preparation he invites his guests to order his specialties — one week in advance, if you please. Such delicacies as stuffed pheasant or medallions of veal with mushrooms are well worth the wait. *Prices:* expensive.

Directions: Leave the Laurentian Autoroute at Exit #67 and proceed east to Route 117 and then north 3 kilometres (2 miles) to l'Auberge de Nice.

La Vieille Ferme de 1900

967, rue Principale
St-Sauveur-des-Monts, Québec
J0R 1R0

Innkeeper: Jules Lalonde
Telephone: 514-227-4766
Credit Cards: All major cards
Facilities: Dining. Fully licensed.
Open year-round, Tuesday to
Sunday.

On a wall of La Vieille Ferme hangs a photograph of Roch Alary, the original owner of the farm. A great photo it is, showing a sturdy pioneer with his two dogs. His weather-beaten face displays the pride of a long, hard life of accomplishment on the farm (he lived from 1898-1974).

At the very young age of 19, Jules Lalonde bought the old house in 1971 and succeeded in restoring and renovating the building to reflect its origins as a pioneer farm. Except for the stone foundation, it is sturdily constructed of wood, and Jules has kept everything as it was, removing only certain partitions to give the dining area a greater feeling of space. Even the gabled second floor has been restored to retain its country look.

The walls are hung with paintings by local artists and with farm artifacts reflecting the building's origins. The simplicity of the house is reflected in Jules's dining philosophy: "We don't serve fancy meals here, just good old-fashioned food with excellent service."

Jules's favourites on the menu are: L'Assiette des délices de la mer — a seafood plate of crabs, scampis, shrimps and scallops cooked in garlic butter and served on a bed of creole rice, and the Filet of sole with nine different vegetables. From his charcoal grill, Jules specializes in Pepper steak with fresh vegetables of the day and

potatoes cooked to your fancy. Jules is quite proud of his Filet Mignon Bouquetière cooked in wine sauce in a bouquet of artichoke, white asparagus, Brussels sprouts, mushrooms and stuffed pepper.

Other items on the menu include scampis, Alaska crab, garlic shrimp on rice and roast beef, the Sunday special. *Prices:* moderate.

For dessert, Jules suggests Pouding au chômeur maison — homemade white cake generously covered in Laurentian maple syrup.

Directions: From Montreal, take the Laurentian Autoroute north to Exit #58, then proceed along rue Principale about 1 kilometre (1/2 mile) beyond the city limits.

❖❖❖❖❖❖❖❖❖❖❖❖❖❖❖❖❖❖❖❖❖❖❖

Le Bistro Illico

1574, rue Bourgogne
Chambly, Québec
J3L 1Y7

Innkeeper: Yvan Pilon
Telephone: 514-658-1048
Credit Cards: MasterCard, Visa, Carte Blanche
Facilities: Dining. Fully licensed. Open year-round. 11:30 a.m. - 1 p.m. (Monday to Friday) 5 p.m. -1 a.m. (Saturday and Sunday)

Chambly is situated on what has been a main north-south invasion route going back to the 17th Century. Fort Chambly was built by the French to guard the fur-trade route and was then used by the British, in 1812, to guard against American invaders.

Over 200 years ago, the site on which Le Bistro Illico sits was actually a farm. A very sturdy barn can still be found behind the restaurant. As Chambly grew, a general store was added, and farmers came from the surrounding countryside to trade their produce for general merchandise. While they were in the store they were provided with a resting and watering place for their horses at the rear of the stable. For many years, the Brien family owned the store and, with the advent of the automobile, installed the famous hand-operated gas pumps that still can be seen here and there.

Because the Richelieu River has direct access to the sea by way of the St. Lawrence, and because of the town's proximity to the U.S.

border, the general store became an outlet for bootleg liquor from the St-Pierre and Miquelon islands during the prohibition era.

In recent years, Yvan Pilon has created a thriving restaurant close to the centre of town, where business people and tourists can have inexpensive but memorable meals. Le Bistro sits right by the river, close to the City Hall and seems to be quite popular. Seating is available on the porch where guests can gaze at all the pleasure boat activity on the river.

Yvan suggested that I lunch on La Baguette Illico. The waitress brought me a very colourful plate made up of a sliced bun with generous portons of ham, salami, mushrooms, tomatoes, green peppers and covered with melted Swiss cheese. On the side were julienne carrots and homefried potatoes — an ample and delicious lunch. For evening dinner, Yvan suggests Lapin à moutarde, Boeuf bourguignon or a ragout of pig's feet. *Prices:* inexpensive.

Directions: Chambly is just a few miles east of Montreal on Route 112, off Route 116.

Le Relais Terrapin

295 ouest, rue St-Charles
Longueuil, Québec
J4H 1E5

Innkeeper: Nassir Kassam
Telephone: 514-677-6378
Credit Cards: All major cards
Facilities: Dining. Lunch: 11 a.m. - 3 p.m. (Mon. to Fri.) Dinner: 4-11 p.m. (Sun. to Mon.) Sunday Brunch: 10 a.m. - 3 p.m. Fully licensed. Open year-round.

Longueuil owes its prominence to the 19th-Century railway barons. It became the western terminus of the Grand Trunk Railways and, as a result, its population boomed. To house and feed the work force that flooded into the area in 1856, Antoine Prévost constructed this former inn close to the railway station. The name Relais Terrapin was chosen in 1880 by its owner, Jay Owens, a Montreal innkeeper.

In 1977, the inn underwent a massive restoration. With its bright, hardwood interior and multiple levels, it has become a lovely, modern restaurant which has retained the atmosphere of its railway past.

Menu specialties include brochette of beef (slices of Filet Mignon served on a bed of rice), rack of lamb, surf 'n turf, poached salmon with hollandaise sauce. An unusual dish is the brochette of scallops wrapped in bacon and served on a bed of rice.

Other items on the very extensive menu include roast chicken in mushroom sauce, escalopes of veal with Dijon mustard, roast beef, and flambéed desserts, such as Crêpes Suzette and Cherries Jubilee. The seafood menu includes Coquille St-Jacques, frog's legs Provençale, and boiled or broiled lobster. *Prices:* inexpensive-to-moderate.

Directions: Longueuil is on the south shore of the St. Lawrence across from downtown Montreal.

❧❧❧❧❧❧❧❧❧❧❧❧❧❧❧❧❧❧❧❧❧❧❧❧❧❧

Le Vieux Moulin

50, rue Faustin
St-Jérôme, Québec
J7Z 3P3

Innkeepers: Denis Mayer and Gerry Legault
Telephone: 514-436-7900
Credit Cards: All major cards
Facilities: Dining. Open year-round, Tuesday to Sunday. Fully licensed. Lunch: 11 a.m. - 2 p.m. (Tuesday to Friday). Dinner: 5-11 p.m.

Le Vieux Moulin is now a delightful inn located on the millrun of la Rivière du Nord as it courses its way through this bustling little town of St-Jérôme at the foothills of the Laurentians. Its history reflects the pattern of settlement of old Quebec from the 18th through to the 20th Century.

From an original French settler, Pierre Auguste Labrie, the island (where the mill now stands) passed into the hands of a Scotsman, Robert Langwell, in 1851. Langwell, who came with the wave of British settlement in the 19th Century, built the flour mill and established a profitable, high-quality milling business. Later, as his fortunes grew, he erected a sawmill behind the existing flour mills.

In 1872, the island and both mills were sold to Louis Brière. At the turn of the century, the entire property and business came under the ownership of the Drouin family, Omer and his son Jules. The Drouin family retained ownership until a devastating fire in 1980.

The mill lost its roof in the fire, but Denis and Gerry managed to save something of the interior and refurbished it as a restaurant and bar. The interior stone walls retain their old grandeur and early photographs of the Drouin family adorn the walls. Bags of Drouin flour can be found in the corners, and the lounge area even has an old Victrola.

One of the nicest parts of the mill is the back porch, almost a boardwalk, overlooking the rapids. Set out there, are some patio tables and chairs where one can enjoy a light lunch in the summer.

Denis tells me that the favourite menu items are Scampis Provençale and Scampis and Filet Mignon, as well as Pepper steak. In addition, the Fondue Bourguignon is delicious. A rather unusual dessert that piqued my interest is the Fondue au Chocolat — fresh fruit dipped into hot, creamy chocolate. *Prices:* moderate.

Directions: Take Exit 44 off the Laurentian Autoroute north from Montreal to St-Jérôme.

❖❖❖❖❖❖❖❖❖❖❖❖❖❖❖❖❖❖❖❖❖❖❖❖❖

Mon Village

2764, côte St-Charles
St-Lazare, Québec
J0P 1V0

Innkeeper: Michael Dobbie
Telephone: 514-458-5331
Credit Cards: MasterCard, Visa, American Express
Facilities: Dining. Fully licensed. Open daily year-round. Lunch: 11:30 a.m. - 2:00 p.m. Dinner: 5:30-10:00 p.m.

Mon Village was the original homestead of Thomas Parsons and his family who arrived from Cumberland, England in 1829. The land was bought from Seigneur Lotbinière of Vaudreuil. Parson's purchase of the land is an example of the changes in ownership that resulted from heavy British immigration to Lower Canada, after the Napoleonic Wars ended in 1815. Many French settlers in the Eastern Townships and the Ottawa Valley sold their properties to eager Englishmen hungry for land in the colonies. The original logs used by Parsons can still be found in the building.

Next door to the restaurant, one of the farm buildings has been converted into a fine bakery. The rolls, bread and pastries served at Mon Village come from here and guests can stock up while visiting the inn.

There are two bars in Mon Village, both very homey and friendly

51

with excellent working fireplaces. The one that struck my fancy was the upstairs pub. Located under a plastered gabled ceiling, its main window, in stained glass, has been fashioned by a local artist and depicts scenes such as skiing and riding to the hounds.

A very extensive menu features: the Parsons' Cut of prime beef loin steaks; the Hodgson's Rib, saluting one of Côte St-Charles's original settlers; Scampis Provençale, nicely seasoned and served on a bed of harvest rice; and Beef 'n Reef, combining choice beef tenderloin and scampis. *Prices:* expensive.

Directions: St-Lazare is a few kilometres south of the Trans-Canada Highway (Route 40) about 40 kilometres west of Montreal.

❖❖❖❖❖❖❖❖❖❖❖❖❖❖❖❖❖❖❖❖❖❖❖❖❖❖❖❖

Parker's Lodge

1340, Chemin Lac-Paquin
Val David, Québec
J0T 2N0

Innkeeper: John R. Parker
Telephone: 819-322-2026
Rooms: 18 (12 with bath)
Rates: (M.A.P.) inexpensive,
weekly packages available.
Facilities: Dining. Swimming,
paddle boats, sailboats, golf,
tennis and skiing nearby. Not
licensed. Open year-round.

I found John Parker in his small office sitting behind his desk, eyes glued to the baseball game on television. After introducing myself, he casually invited me to look around and help myself — all without looking up once! It was clear that sports had a high priority in the life of the inn.

As I wandered around the lodge, I realized that it was the expression of Parker's personality. It is quiet, unpretentious and very homey. All the rooms, both public and private, have simple Québécois furniture on hardwood floors covered by traditional braided rugs. Its most imposing feature is the panoramic view of Lac-Paquin from the rear verandah. The living room has a warm, cosy ambience about it — comfortable chairs, lots of books and an equally great view of the lake.

After completing my tour, I was able to ascertain from John that the lodge was first built in 1910 and had only four rooms. John and his late wife took over in 1944, making continual additions along the way. Many of his guests have been returning for 25 years and have become good friends, which is a great tribute to John and his quiet lodge.

Meals are served family style around large oval tables. If you wish merely to have dinner, John will include you amongst his guests for a simple meal of his specialties, quiche and berry pies. *Prices:* inexpensive.

Directions: From the Laurentian Autoroute, take Exit #80 and proceed west on rue Lac-Paquin approximately half a kilometre (one-quarter mile) to Parker's Lodge.

Restaurant à l'Étang des Moulins

888, rue St-Louis
Terrebonne, Québec
J6W 1K1

Innkeeper: Jean Cayer
Telephone: 514-471-4018
Credit Cards: All major cards
Facilities: Dining. Open year-round, Wednesday to Sunday. Fully licensed. Lunch: 11 a.m. - 3 p.m. (Wed. to Fri.) Dinner: 6-11 p.m.

Restaurant à l'Étang des Moulins (at the Mill Pond) is aptly named. It sits at the corner of rue St-Louis and boulevard des Braves. On one side is the mill powered by la Rivière des Milles Îles and behind is the lovely pond with a small park overlooking it. On the afternoon of my visit, a flock of geese had commandeered the pond and were allowing some children to feed them bread.

As I was admiring this scene, I met Jacques Tremblay, former owner of the building that houses the restaurant. Upon learning of my interest, he insisted on taking me into his home next door to relate the colourful history of the two buildings' owners.

The most famous owner of the buildings was Joseph-Alfred Duschenau, who obtained the house as a result of a sheriff's sale in 1870. Later, he was an unsuccessful Liberal politician and still later prefect of the now infamous St-Vincent de Paul penitentiary. He also became the mayor of Terrebonne.

Jean Cayer has owned the building since November 1982. Jean has added a nice feature — a patio at the back of the house. How nice it must be to sit out on a warm summer afternoon overlooking the park and pond.

The menu includes Feuilleté des cuisses de grenouille (frog's legs wrapped in pastry); Coquille de fruits de mer (assorted seafoods on the half-shell); and Rognons de veau au Porto (veal kidneys in wine sauce). Desserts include Gateau au Cointreau and Panache of sherbet. *Prices:* moderate.

Directions: From Montreal, take the Laurentian Autoroute north to Exit #20, then proceed east on Route 640, 28 kilometres (17 miles) to Terrebonne.

Restaurant Phidimus

875, rue St-Francis Xavier
Terrebonne, Québec
J6W 1K1

Innkeeper: Roland Martineau
Telephone: 514-471-0115
Credit Cards: MasterCard, Visa
Facilities: Dining. Fully licensed.
Open year-round, Tuesday to
Sunday. Lunch: 11 a.m. - 3 p.m.
(Tuesday to Friday). Dinner:
5 p.m. - 1 a.m.

In the 1830s a Yorkshire blacksmith, Matthew Moody, bought the building, which now houses Restaurant Phidimus, and proceeded to turn it into a farm machinery factory. So successful did Moody become that his equipment was known far and wide for its quality and value. To accommodate the increase in business he bought the house next door and even opened another factory, just west of Terrebonne.

According to a pamphlet entitled *Vieux Terrebonne* (Old Terrebonne), the architecture of the building is truly representative of the style of the region during the 17th and 18th Centuries. Its small size, gabled roof, dormer windows and walls, white plastered inside and out, lend it a simple, functional and attractive appearance. Roland

Martineau, the innkeeper, spent a few minutes showing me both the intimate 'Canadienne' interior and the inviting summer patio out back. The restaurant's kitchen is simple with early Québec antiques throughout.

The menu reflects French-Canadian specialties. The favourites are Lapin à l'estragon (rabbit with tarragon), Escalope de veau porte-feuille, the traditional Tourtière du Lac-St-Jean (pork pie) and Jambon à l'érable (ham with maple sauce). Seafood items include Pétoncles sautées au gin (liquor-flavoured scallops) and Crêpe de fruits de mer.

Desserts include carrot cake, sugar cake in cream and apple tarts. *Prices:* moderate.

Directions: From Montreal, take the Laurentian Autoroute north to Exit #20, then proceed east on route 640, 28 kilometres (17 miles) to Terrebonne.

❖❖❖❖❖❖❖❖❖❖❖❖❖❖❖❖❖❖❖❖❖❖

Willow Inn

208 Main Road
Como, Québec
J0P 1A0

Innkeeper: David Crockart
Telephone: 514-458-7006
Rooms: 8 (all with bath)
Rates: inexpensive (includes continental breakfast)
Credit Cards: MasterCard, Visa, American Express
Facilities: Dining. Fully licensed. Open year-round.

This comfortable inn just outside of Montreal was originally a general store around 1820. The owner, George Malette, sold it sometime later to Francois-Xavier Desjardins, who became an organizer of "Patriotes" and fought in the Rebellion of 1837-38. Apparently, he was arrested by the British, but let go. Perhaps in gratitude he became a Captain in the loyal militia.

David Crockart now presides over this friendly hostelry. We had dinner on the porch, overlooking the beautiful Lake of Two Mountains. My friend ordered a perfect Filet Mignon which came wrapped in bacon and a delicious garlic sauce. I was served a monstrous portion of Prime ribs of beef with baked potato and vegetables.

Another specialty of the menu is Brome Lake duckling pie stuffed with fresh apples and herb dressing, with a sauce of apple Brandy and Laurentian maple syrup — a marvellous treat. *Prices:* moderate.

Of course, dessert would not be dessert without a serving of English trifle or Oka Cheese from the famous Oka monastery situated just across the water.

The inn also has a very cosy English pub complete with two fireplaces which produce a warm glow during the chilly autumn and winter days. One can also play darts or merely converse amiably with friends while enjoying a cool brew. The Pub serves light meals, including something called the Willow Inn Dunk, which is a hot roast beef sandwich with a piquant sauce. Also available is the Croque Monsieur, an open-faced sandwich with melted cheese, tomatoes, mushrooms and green peppers on back bacon.

Directions: From the Trans-Canada Highway (Route 40), take Exit #26 west of Dorion and proceed along Route 342 to Bellevue Road. Turn right on Main Road, then left to the Willow Inn.

Eastern Townships & Beauce

The Eastern Townships were first settled by the United Empire Loyalists who would not participate in the American Revolution of 1776 and remained loyal to the British Crown. Also, after the Civil War of 1861-5, many wealthy Southerners who used to summer in New England spurned Yankee territory for the Quebec countryside. Thus, though Quebec is predominantly French Canadian, there are still little villages here and there where the population is mostly English Canadian — fascinating contrasts which abound in the province.

Now the Eastern Townships is rich dairy country and a tourist paradise. Mount Orford and Sutton are two of the famous ski areas. In the summer, the area abounds with all the sports facilities plus great opportunities for finding crafts, antiques, and summer theatre.

The Chaudière Valley is the heart of Beauce country, now a beautiful drive. However, in 1776 it was the highway of American invasion led by Benedict Arnold. The 200th anniversary of this invasion was celebrated in the town of St-Georges in 1975. Today this same route, Route 173, from the Maine border is called President Kennedy Highway to commemorate him and the historic comradeship of our two peoples.

Eastern Townships

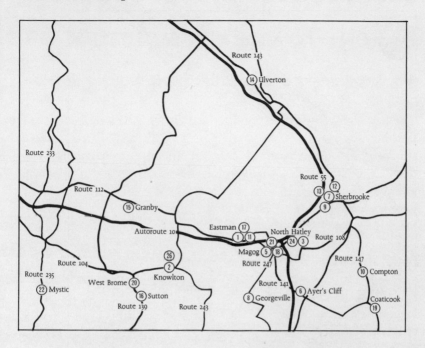

Beauce

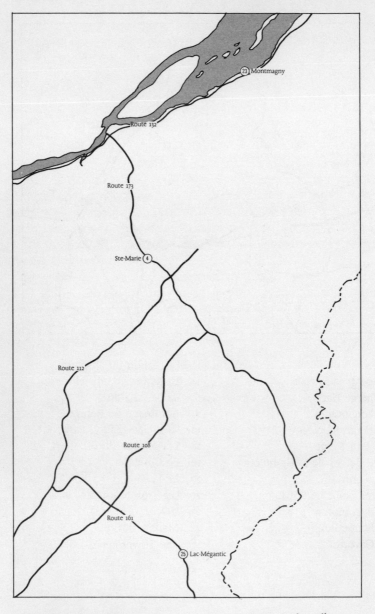

4 Auberge La Seigneurie   25 Restaurant La Chapelle
23 Manoir des Érables

Auberge du Fenil

R.R. #1
Chemin Mont Bon Plaisir
Eastman, Québec
JoE 1P0

Innkeeper: Jacques Robert
Telephone: 514-297-3362
Rooms: 18 (all with bath)
Rates: (M.A.P.) inexpensive
Credit Cards: MasterCard, Visa,
American Express, En Route
Facilities: Dining, outdoor pool,
tennis, cross-country and alpine
skiing. Fully licensed.

As Jacques was showing me around this rustic inn, he referred me to the former owner of the farm, Roger Blanchard, who lived nearby and who could relate the history of the inn. Roger's grandfather, Joseph, owned the property which was passed down through the family until Roger sold it for development in 1965. At that time, the up-to-date inn was added to the cattle barn that already existed.

While Jacques and I walked around, he pointed to the duck pond where six ducks were placidly swimming around. "There are supposed to be seven ducks," he said, "but one is on vacation."

The accommodations are located in a new building and are decorated in early Québécois style and are extremely comfortable. Downstairs is a cosy living room with a nice fireplace to warm up the skiers after their day on the slopes.

Montreal Magazine, in a review of l'Auberge du Fenil said, "Belying its cosy informality, Fenil's kitchen is hardnosed uptown." Jacques' table d'hôte favourites are Dandine de canard à l'érable, the traditional rabbit à l'Ancienne, Escalope of veal in cream and scampis du Fenil on a bed of rice. *Prices:* expensive.

Directions: Leave Autoroute 10 at exit #106 at Eastman.

❖❖❖❖❖❖❖❖❖❖❖❖❖❖❖❖❖❖❖❖❖❖❖❖❖❖❖

Auberge du Relais

30, rue Knowlton
Knowlton, Québec
J0E 1V0

Innkeeper: Gaston Letourneau
Telephone: 514-243-6136
Rooms: 12 (3 shared baths)
Rates: very inexpensive
Credit Cards: All major cards
Facilities: Dining. Fully licensed.
Open year-round. Alpine and
cross-country skiing, antiquing,
craft shops nearby.

The fact that l'Auberge du Relais remains an inn at all is a result of two flukes of history. The Tavern Files of the Brome County Historical Society Archives tell us that the stage coach route was

changed in bygone days to go through to Magog, which resulted in the railway following the same route. Had both these historical events not come to pass, the Auberge du Relais would probably be a grocery store today. However, as luck would have it, the Kimball family built this inn which grew and prospered over the years.

Today the inn stands as a resting place for those who are interested more in the tourist attractions of the surrounding area than in luxurious comforts. This simple but comfortable establishment is a fine place for those who want to ski all the great hills in the area or would like to tour the back roads looking for antiques and crafts or who just want to take in the spectacular scenery.

Over a cup of coffee, Gaston told me that the two favourite menu items were barbecued duck (the famous Brome Lake duckling) and pepper steak à L'Armagnac. However, his great pride was in fresh grilled lobster and Assiette de pêcheur (fisherman's platter) including lobster, scampis, frog's legs, crabs and scallops for two. Other selections include steak, surf 'n turf, escalope of veal, sole and rainbow trout. *Prices:* moderate.

Directions: Leave Autoroute 10 at Exit #90. Proceed south on Route 243, 12 kilometres (7 miles) to Knowlton.

❧❧❧❧❧❧❧❧❧❧❧❧❧❧❧❧❧❧❧❧❧❧

Auberge Hatley

Route Magog
North Hatley, Québec
J0B 2C0

Innkeepers: Liliane and Robert Gagnon
Telephone: 819-842-2325
Rooms: 20 (all with bath)
Rates: moderate
Credit Cards: MasterCard, Visa
Facilities: Dining, indoor pool, lake swimming, sailing and boating, cross-country and downhill skiing nearby. Open year-round. Fully licensed.

This whole area of southeastern Quebec has close ties to the United States. It was the scene of an American invasion after the American Revolution in 1776. It became home for many from the 13 colonies who remained loyal to the Crown in the 1780s; and, after the Civil

War, many wealthy southerners who used to vacation in New England could no longer spend their time in the despised Yankee Territory so they began to build summer homes in this area.

This auberge was the original home of John Holt, founder of Holt Renfrew stores. Holt was one of many wealthy Montrealers who summered in the area after the completion of the railway to the Townships. Over a hundred years later, vacationers now have a chance to enjoy this gracious home with its magnificent view of the lake and countryside under the capable stewardship of Liliane and Robert Gagnon.

Over coffee, we talked in front of the fireplace of the former living room. I noticed two huge iron pots sitting on the ground near the swimming pool, and asked what they were for. "Oh, we just light them for effect during the evenings," Liliane said. "But every Wednesday we barbecue a whole lamb in that outdoor spit over there."

All the rooms are filled with genuine antiques of the mid-19th Century which adds considerably to the rich décor.

The excitement occasioned by the setting and the inn itself is heightened considerably by the presence of Guy Bohec, a Canadian chef. Guy has been on a number of Canadian culinary teams and has been chosen to go to the 1984 World Food Olympics in Frankfurt. In addition, Montreal's prestigious food magazine *Sel et Poivre* chose the inn as a feature in one of their issues.

The table d'hôte menu has hors d'oeuvres made of such things as parfait of fish, seafood in yogurt sauce, and avocado and mushroom salad in cream and blueberry vinegar. The main course features such delicacies as baby salmon in asparagus sauce stuffed with mashed mushrooms and the unusual medallion of veal in grapefruit sauce. After that sumptuous banquet, Guy serves the traditional Gâteau d'Auberge, a rum and maple cake.

Directions: From Autoroute 10, take Exit #121 to Route 55. Proceed south to Exit #29 and take Route 108 east 12 kilometres (7 miles) to North Hatley.

❧❧❧❧❧❧❧❧❧❧❧❧❧❧❧❧❧❧❧❧❧❧❧❧

Auberge La Seigneurie

700 nord, rue Notre-Dame
Ste-Marie, Beauce, Québec
G0S 2Y0

Innkeeper: Cyrille Dulac
Telephone: 418-387-2607
Rooms: 29 (all with bath)
Rates: very inexpensive
Credit Cards: MasterCard, Visa, American Express
Facilities: Dining. Fully licensed. Indoor pool, sauna. Open year-round.

La Seigneurie refers to the parcel of land granted to Jacques Thomas Taschereau by the King of France in 1735. Still standing across the road from the inn is the stunning white-columned Manor House built by Taschereau. In 1955, his descendant, Remy, assembled a number of buildings on the former seigneurie to create the small and comfortable inn which bears its name. He can relate colourful stories of his family's past, including that of a newspaper editor jailed by the British for disloyalty. Other ancestors have included the first Cardinal of Canada, a Premier of the province and a judge of the Supreme Court of Canada.

In 1975, the town of Ste-Marie was also the site for the bicentenary of Benedict Arnold's American invasion into Beauce country. His descendants arrived decked out in 1775 military costume and were greeted, this time at least, with a more traditional holiday welcome.

Rooms are simply done and very inexpensive.

The dining room boasts a wide selection of dishes: Château Brillion for two, Beefsteak with Dijon sauce, slices of ham flavoured with pineapple, Salmon steak and Filet of sole à la Meunière. *Prices:* moderate.

Directions: From Sherbrooke, proceed east on Route 112, 150 kilometres (93 miles) to Vallée Jonction. Turn north on Route 173, 10 kilometres (6 miles) to Ste-Marie. From Quebec City, drive south on Route 173, 50 kilometres (36 miles).

❖❖❖❖❖❖❖❖❖❖❖❖❖❖❖❖❖❖❖❖❖❖❖❖❖

Auberge Orford

20 sud, rue Merry
Magog, Québec
J1K 3K9

Innkeeper: Alfred Pelletier
Telephone: 819-843-9361
Rooms: 13 (9 with bath)
Rates: inexpensive
Credit Cards: MasterCard, Visa, American Express
Facilities: Dining. Fully licensed.

I was sitting on the porch of L'Auberge Orford, overlooking the outdoor patio and the marina on the Magog River, talking to Alfred Pelletier when he calmly told me that this hundred-year-old building once housed a mortuary. As I looked furtively around, he reassured

me, "I think there are no more bodies around, but I haven't really checked." I didn't offer to help him either. Alfred told me of one patron who sat in the bar all evening literally crying in his beer because the last time he was there was to visit his father who had just passed away. The people of Magog have now become accustomed to Auberge's new identity, and the warmth and charm of Alfred and his staff certainly contribute to its ambience.

The thirteen rooms are furnished simply but comfortably, some giving a nice view of the activity on the river.

During the summer, Alfred puts on a well-advertised Méchou. A two-hundred-pound hindquarter of beef is barbecued on an open spit all day, giving off the delicious aroma to passersby, advertising the feast to come that evening.

I was fortunate to lunch on the porch, l'Estrienne, and was served a filling salad of egg, cheese, ham, onions, tomatoes and lobster.

Dinner offers a table d'hôte selection of barbecued steaks, chicken and salmon. *Prices:* moderate.

Directions: Magog is approximately 120 kilometres (75 miles) east of Montreal on Autoroute 10, Exits #118 or #120.

❧❧❧❧❧❧❧❧❧❧❧❧❧❧❧❧❧❧❧

Auberge Ripplecove

Ayer's Cliff, Québec
JoB 1Co

Innkeeper: Stephen Stafford
Telephone: 819-838-4296
Rooms: 11 (all with bath); 8 chalets
Rates: (M.A.P.) inexpensive-to-expensive
Credit Cards: MasterCard, Visa, American Express
Facilities: Dining, tennis, outdoor pool, lake swimming, windsurfing, cross-country skiing. Alpine skiing and golf nearby. Open year-round. Fully licensed.

Ripplecove Inn is built on the site of the Clough farm, which dates back to the early 1800s. The Cloughs were part of the early United Empire Loyalist settlement in the Eastern Townships. As a reminder of those days, there sits on the property an old log cabin, formerly a maple syrup cabin, that now houses a group of up to 8 people.

In 1870, Mr. Ayer, after whom the town was named, donated lots to the railway to encourage an extension north from the U.S. border to Sherbrooke. A flood of wealthy Americans arrived who set up their magnificent villas. Many inns were later built to service the burgeoning tourist trade. By 1900, there were more than fifteen inns in the area.

The Ripplecove Inn, always owned by the Stafford family, was destroyed in a tragic fire in 1978. The family recreated this charming year-round resort which includes a number of housekeeping units.

One of the features of the Inn is the Anchorage Dining Room and Bar. This bar is truly unusual as a replica of the Hampden Traveller of early Nova Scotia. I was sitting in the lounge, next to the bar, admiring the fireplace and the nautical ambience of the dining room, and Francine Leroux explained that the nautical motif was chosen in recognition of their specialty — seafood.

The menu sparkles with such items as the Ripplecove Trawler, which is a blend of charcoal-broiled beef and seafood pan sautéed for two. Live lobster from Nova Scotia is boiled or grilled and served with a lemon wedge and melted garlic or drawn butter. In addition to scampis, shrimp and Alaska snow crab, other selections include pepper steak flambé and sautéed in butter with peppercorn sauce, and rack of lamb charcoal broiled with a unique Ripplecove Sauce. *Prices:* moderate-to-expensive.

Directions: Leave Autoroute 10 at Exit #121, proceed south on Route 55 for 16 kilometres (10 miles) to Exit #21, then take Route 141 a few miles east to Ayer's Cliff.

❀❀❀❀❀❀❀❀❀❀❀❀❀❀❀❀❀❀❀❀❀❀❀❀❀❀❀

Au P'tit Sabot

1410 ouest, rue King
Sherbrooke, Québec
J1J 2C2

Innkeeper: Guy Larente
Telephone: 819-563-0262
Credit Cards: MasterCard, Visa
Facilities: Dining. Fully licensed.
Open year-round, Tuesday to Sunday.

Dick van Bloudorr, an immigrant from Holland, is the source of the history of this charming little restaurant at Sherbrooke's west end. A conversation with him reveals that around the turn of the century, a Monsieur Goyette opened a grocery store on this site. His chief claim to fame was that he gave candies to the kids. Some of the restaurant customers have a fond memory of dear old Monsieur Goyette and his candies.

After Goyette gave up his business, the building was used as a snack bar. In 1970, van Bloudorr bought it. He named it after a Dutch symbol — the little wooden shoe. He also added a façade to give the restaurant the appearance of a house.

Le P'tit Sabot has justly earned its fame as a restaurant of distinction in Sherbrooke. Guy Larente has had forty years of experience as a chef, having worked both at the Seigneury Club near Ottawa and at Toronto's Royal York Hotel. Guy, Simonne and their whole family strive to provide a warm atmosphere along with some very delicious food.

Guy indicated to me that his menu favourites were Sanglier de l'Estrie — wild boar à la Eastern Townships, sweetbreads in cream, and pheasant with Bourguignon pears. Additionally, Guy serves Escalopes of veal à la Dijonnaise, rabbit à la Eastern Townships with rice pilaf, pepper steak and brochette of Filet Mignon with rice pilaf. From the seafood menu, the standards are Frog's Legs Provençale and Crab's Legs Provençale. *Prices:* expensive.

Sunday brunch, which Guy and Simonne call "La petite folie du dimanche", included Eggs Benedict, sausage, ham, bacon or crepes.

Directions: Sherbrooke is 150 kilometres (93 miles) east of Montreal, just off Autoroute 10 and Route 55.

Aux Berges
de la Grand'ourse

Route 247
Georgeville, Québec
JoB 1To

Innkeeper: Roch Nadeau
Telephone: 819-843-8636
Rooms: 11 (3 shared baths)
Rates: (M.A.P.) inexpensive
Credit Cards: MasterCard
Facilities: Dining, skiing, tennis.
Fully licensed. Open Wednesday
to Sunday in summer; weekends
only in winter.

I must say that for me a visit to Georgeville was one of strange contrast. Here, in southeastern Quebec is a little village almost totally English-Canadian. The storekeeper at the General Store was an Anglophone. Everyone I spoke to was anglophone. Everything in it, that is except Roch Nadeau who prefers to speak French. In addition, there is no doubt that this inn is Québécois to the core. Fleurs de Lys flags are everywhere in evidence and the rooms are named after such famous modern Quebec heroes as Robert Cliche, now a judge; other rooms are named after Quebec poets and artists.

Georgeville was originally named after George Copps, son of the first ferry owner on Lake Memphremagog, home of the dreaded Anaconda, monster of Memphremagog. It was the site of a village of fine Georgian-style frame homes. Among them was the fishing lodge founded by Lena and Doug McGowan who ran the lodge for forty-five years. Prior to the roads being built, the Montreal élite would take the train to Magog, then board the *Anthemis* for the short ferry ride to Georgeville.

La Grand'ourse (the Big Dipper) signifies regional Québécois cuisine and that is certainly what Roch Nadeau is providing. The menu features stuffed piglet with white cranberry sauce with zucchini and red cabbage in beer, Flemish style. Also served is the indispensable Canard de Lac-Brome, a standard dish in the Eastern Townships along with famous cheeses from the nearby monastery of St-Benoît. Meals by reservation only. *Prices:* expensive.

Directions: Leave Autoroute 10 at Magog and proceed south on Route 247, 16 kilometres (10 miles) to Georgeville.

❖❖❖❖❖❖❖❖❖❖❖❖❖❖❖❖❖❖❖❖❖❖❖❖❖

Da Toni

45 nord, rue Wellington
Sherbrooke, Québec
J1H 5B5

Innkeeper: Toni Danella
Telephone: 819-567-8441
Credit Cards: All major cards
Facilities: Dining. Open year round. Fully licensed.

Around the turn of the century, on the site of 45, rue Wellington rose the Sherbrooke branch of La Banque Canadienne Nationale. In 1968, it was sold to Toni who recreated the interior to resemble a Gothic monastery, complete with torches bracketed to the walls. It is indeed an impressive introduction. I almost expected to be greeted by cassocked monks in sandals, but instead a formal hostess took me to my table. As I sat there taking in the surroundings, it occurred to me that Toni, in his way, has been carrying on the tradition exemplified by the bank. They were a repository of public savings and as such were an institution of trust. For six years, he has kept a trust by bringing the cuisine of Northern Italy to Quebec, with a promise to maintain the quality for his patrons. If the meal that I ate is any indication, he has more than fulfilled his trust.

I asked Toni what he would suggest, and in a few minutes a piping hot dish of Scampis flambéed with cognac appeared, which was a gourmet's delight. The restaurant specializes in veal — Veal à la Romance, Cordon Bleu, Saltinbocca, and Scaloppini. Chicken cacciatore, Dover sole belle meunière with lemon sauce, mushrooms and tomatoes are some of the other features. *Prices:* inexpensive.

Directions: Sherbrooke is 150 kilometres (93 miles) east of Montreal, off Route 55 and from Autoroute 10.

Hôtel Domaine Saint-Laurent de Compton

C.P. 180
Compton, Québec
J0B 1L0

Innkeeper: Gérard St-Laurent
Telephone: 819-835-5464
Rooms: 175 (all with bath)
Rates: very inexpensive-to-expensive
Credit Cards: MasterCard, Visa, American Express
Facilities: Dining, tennis, indoor pool, sauna, whirlpool. Riding school, fishing, cross-country skiing nearby. Open year-round. Fully licensed.

Domaine Saint-Laurent certainly is an appropriate name for this resort in the small village of Compton, a few miles south of Sherbrooke. Compton was the birthplace of Canada's Prime Minister Louis St. Laurent who is buried in the cemetery here. The Domaine is actually a huge complex comprised of a former school and residences for the girls who once attended King's Hall, first erected in 1874.

For me, the key to appreciating the past, present and future of the Domaine is to visit the small bar near the dining room and to take a walk among the villas springing up in the countryside a few yards away from the main complex. The furniture in the bar is made up of old school desks with the girls' graffiti etched across them. "I hate lessons" was a common inscription. The walls are hung with photographs of the girls in their various activities, field hockey being the one that stuck in my mind. Fernande, Gérard's wife, tells me that many of the former students return as guests of the Domaine and are drawn to this bar, perhaps to see themselves or their friends.

The future is embodied in the villas. Here is a concept unique in North America. Investors are invited to participate in the expansion of the Domaine by buying a villa of four to six suites. These units are managed by Gérard and his team. In return, the owner receives a large percentage of the revenue. Thus, the investor is happy, he can achieve a nice return on his investment because of the minimum occupancy required, and Gérard is happy because he has increased his capacity at no cost.

Gillard Hall is the old school residence comprising 84 rooms and 4 wings. All the rooms have been modernized to include bathrooms and they afford simple comfortable accommodations.

This whole bustling Domaine is under the quiet stewardship of Gérard and his team. He is a gentle, kind man who puts in inhuman hours making sure that his guests are enjoying themselves while still taking the time to join them for a drink or dinner.

The favourites of the fine cuisine are sirloin steak Domaine, rack of lamb with fine herbs and scampis grilled with garlic butter. Other items on the menu include Chateaubriand Bouquetière, Surf 'n Turf, King Crab and Filet of sole with white wine sauce. *Prices:* moderate-to-expensive.

Directions: From Sherbrooke proceed south on Route 143, then Route 147 from Lennoxville for 16 kilometres (10 miles) to Compton.

La Bonne Bouffe

233, rue Principale
Eastman, Québec
J0E 1C0

Innkeepers: Claude and Thérèse Guindon
Telephone: 514-297-2420
Credit Cards: MasterCard, Visa
Facilities: Dining. Open year-round, Tuesday to Sunday. Fully licensed. Dinner: 5 p.m. - 11 p.m.

On the main street of the small village of Eastman sits a gem of a restaurant, La Bonne Bouffe. I arrived there for dinner, early one Sunday evening, and very quickly the place filled up. I asked Thérèse to serve me what she would recommend and what a feast she served. As a starter, I was treated to a pheasant pâté in pastry that just

melted in my mouth. The main course, Le Feuilleté de Fruits de mer Gratinée, made up of small pieces of lobster, crab, scallops, clams, mushrooms and shrimps, is indescribably delicious.

Claude began his chef's career at the famous Alpine Inn in the Laurentians and his training certainly has stood him in good stead. He takes such care with each meal that he cautions his guests, "All our meals not precooked and require special attention. Please be patient." His careful preparation produces delicacies such as a fourteen-ounce rib steak, filet mignon au Marsala with wine and mushroom sauce, broiled scampis in garlic butter and broiled lobster tails. *Prices:* moderate-to-expensive.

La Bonne Bouffe was, for a hundred years, the headquarters of the local Caisse Populaire, and its low beam ceilings and white plastered walls are reminiscent of a small café of France.

Directions: Leave Autoroute 10 at Exit #106 which takes you into Eastman, about 103 kilometres (64 miles) east of Montreal.

⚜⚜⚜⚜⚜⚜⚜⚜⚜⚜⚜⚜⚜⚜⚜⚜⚜⚜⚜⚜

La Gavotte

365 est, rue King
Sherbrooke, Québec
J1G 1B3

Innkeeper: Louis Le Gall
Telephone: 819-566-6622
Credit Cards: MasterCard, Visa, American Express
Facilities: Dining. Fully licensed. Open year-round, Tuesday to Saturday.

As I walked into La Gavotte, I was struck by a gallery of stunning black and white photographs, mostly of maritime scenes. As I looked around further, I noticed a flag that I had never seen before. "That's the flag of Brittany," Annie Le Gall said. I was quickly informed that La Gavotte is a Breton folk dance, and that the restaurant, of course, has a Breton theme. Annie herself is from Brittany and returns there every year to visit her family.

La Gavotte was originally built in the 1880s by the Martin family as a private residence. As the years passed, additions were made and, in the 1920s, it became a grocery store with the Morgan family (descendants of the Martins) living upstairs.

In the 1940s, nurses from the St. Vincent de Paul Hospital across the street used to gather there every afternoon to exchange gossip.

Mrs. Morgan soon began to provide them delicious cakes and cookies to go along with their tea and gossip.

The simple handwritten menu belies the sophistication of the food. Annie and her chef-husband provide such delicacies as La Feuilleté de fruit de mer, which is a fluffy pastry filled with seafood; scampis à la crême in pastry; the traditional Québécois civet du lapin in white wine and a rather imaginative dish — boned quail with raspberry vinegar in cream sauce. Of course, one can also order the famous Matane shrimps à la Provençale.

The menu also sparkles with Brochette of marinated lamb and slice of duck breast with green pepper. *Prices:* moderate.

Directions: Sherbrooke is off Autoroute 10 and Route 55, approximately 150 kilometres (93 miles) east of Montreal.

La Maison du Spaghetti

208 est, rue King
Sherbrooke, Québec
J1G 1A6

Innkeepers: Monique and Jean-Jacques Lamoureux
Telephone: 819-566-4117
Credit Cards: MasterCard, Visa, American Express
Facilities: Dining. Open daily year-round. Fully licensed.

If La Maison du Spaghetti brings to mind thoughts of just another house, banish those thoughts immediately. Monique and Jean-Jacques, in two short years, have transformed this stately Victorian mansion into a very fine restaurant. To celebrate the 80th anniversary of the home, they created a total of 80 different selections: 20 spaghettis, 20 brochettes, 20 salads and 20 wines.

In 1906, Herménégilde Hébert, future mayor of Sherbrooke, built this fine mansion as a family home. In those days, it was the custom in Sherbrooke for French and English mayors to alternate every two years. When Herménégilde was not mayor, he made his living as a wholesale fruit merchant storing his fruit in the cool basement of his house.

The last owner, prior to Monique and Jean-Jacques, was Dr. Roméo Veilleux. He situated himself well — next door is the St. Vincent de Paul Hospital which allows Jean-Jacques to boast, "None of my customers go to the hospital but many of their customers come to me."

Besides being a fine doctor, Veilleux was also an avid horse player. Jean-Jacques tells me that many of his customers fondly remember coming to visit the good doctor, not as a patient, but as a fellow horse-racing fan.

Monique and Jacques have shown their respect for the historical value of their building by preserving all the old woodwork, including a beautiful balustrade and some stained glass windows. As Monique has said, "It is essential to protect the original character of the house."

My dinner consisted of a starter Trempette de crudités, made up of carrots, celery, cucumber and mushrooms with a delicious dip. I then followed with Jean-Jacques' favourite Brochette de Fruits de Mer consisting of deliciously prepared small pieces of lobster, scallops, shrimps and mushrooms surrounded by vegetables, set on a bed of rice. The favourite is l'Artiste, with pepperoni, crispy vegetables and mushrooms, all grated.

77

I finished off with 1906 coffee, a special blend of three liqueurs and two coffees, named to commemorate the date of the Maison's construction. *Prices:* moderate.

Directions: Sherbrooke is off Autoroute 10 and Route 55, approximately 150 kilometres (93 miles) east of Montreal.

La Maison Wadleigh

Route 143
Ulverton, Québec
J0B 2B0

Innkeeper: Michel Du Pré
Telephone: 819-826-3219
Credit Cards: MasterCard, Visa
Facilities: Dining. Open year-round, Wednesday to Sunday. Fully licensed. Dinner: 5:30-10 p.m.

As I drove into Ulverton, I noticed two churches, both Protestant. Ulverton, it seems, is an anomaly of the Eastern Townships — an English-Canadian town. English and French live here as neighbours in a quiet little village that was once almost completely English. It has become so important to preserve villages like this that the Provincial Government has generously helped the citizens to maintain them. The nearby Moulin Blanchette has been completely restored and is open to the public as living testament to its 19th-Century beginnings.

In 1885, Mr. Wadleigh, an immigrant from the United States, settled in Ulverton and in very short order owned four or five farms in the region. He opened a general store in the village and as a tangible expression of his status in the community, he started to build a grand two-storey house. His neighbours and friends urged him to add a third storey so that his house would be truly unique.

Wadleigh paid those who were building his house a grand sum of $1.25 a day, but also provided them with fine meals. So began the tradition of serving the public that finds its expression in the excellent cuisine that Michel serves to the increasing number of guests that come from near and far.

La Maison serves a seven-course table d'hôte dinner. It was my good fortune to start off with the onion soup followed by mushroom caps stuffed with snails, and shrimps with garlic sauce. The main course was a delicious steak with six different peppers. My dessert was Strawberry Parfait. It was a most memorable meal.

The menu changes weekly, but one can usually find scallops in lemon sauce, rabbit stew, filet of veal à l'Estragon and chicken supreme with lobster sauce. *Prices:* expensive.

Directions: From Sherbrooke, take Route 143 north to Ulverton. From Montreal, take Autoroute 20 to Drummondville, then proceed south on Route 143.

La Petite Suisse

33, rue St-Joseph
Granby, Québec
J2G 6T6

Innkeeper: Adrien Burgdorfer
Telephone: 514-372-7733
Credit Cards: MasterCard, Visa,
American Express
Facilities: Dining. Open year-
round. Fully licensed. Lunch:
11:30 a.m. - 2 p.m. (Tues to Fri)
Dinner: 5-11:30 p.m. (Tues to
Sun)

Granby has been the home of Adrien Burgdorfer since 1951 when he started a food importing business. In 1980, he decided with his wife, Solange, to bring his experience with food into the restaurant business. Thus, Granby now boasts one of the finest restaurants east of Montreal.

Over 75 years ago, this was the site of the first primary school in Granby serving the parish of l'église Notre-Dame. It passed through many hands until it became the unique restaurant with the Swiss motif.

The windows and restaurant are decorated with bells and geraniums and Adrien explained that these are the Swiss folklore signs of welcome. He is well equipped to offer a fine welcome, having been honoured as a *Chevalier de la Croix de Manoir*.

The restaurant indeed looks like a small Swiss inn, and Adrien, who came upon his culinary ability by chance, ("I just realized that I was a born cook") serves a fine selection of dishes. A Swiss restaurant cannot get by without fondues and Adrien tells me that his specialty is Fondue Neuchâteloise. From the grill, he recommends Tournedos vegetable bouquetière, as well as Veal cutlets Viennese, and Raclette Valaisienne. Among the seafood, filet of perch belle meunière and frog's legs Provençale are favourites. *Prices:* moderate.

Directions: Granby is halfway between Montreal and Sherbrooke on Route 112, just off Autoroute 10.

❈❈❈❈❈❈❈❈❈❈❈❈❈❈❈❈❈❈❈❈❈❈❈❈❈

L'Auberge du Refuge

33, rue Maple
Sutton, Québec
JoE 2K0

Innkeepers: Patrice and Lise Falluel
Telephone: 514-538-3802
Rooms: 13 (4 shared baths)
Rates: very inexpensive-to-expensive
Credit Cards: MasterCard, Visa, American Express
Facilities: Dining. Open year-round, weekends only May, June, October, November. Close to excellent skiing, antiquing and theatre. Fully licensed.

For those who enjoy the activities of the Eastern Townships in summer or winter and are interested in truly unusual food, L'Auberge du Refuge should not be missed. The simple accommodations are geared for those active souls who like to get out on their skis or just dash around the back roads of Quebec.

The thick stand of forest in the area attracted the Thomson family from Scotland who erected a sawmill here in 1840. Next door, they built their private residence which Patrice and Lise have converted into a comfortable country inn.

Patrice, who trained in France in hotel and restaurant management, creates the food delicacies, while Lise is responsible for the décor. All the macramé wallhangings, drapes, lamp shades and batiks are her creation, as well as the unusual use of aquariums as table bases and bar. It is very unusual to be sitting at a table and be confronted by colourful fish swimming around and looking placidly up at you. As Patrice put it, "This is a nice conversation piece and above all, no noise."

Patrice has created a number of equally unusual dishes, specializing in, but not restricted to crêpes. The most popular crêpe dish is Crêpe Cabana with seafood, béchamel, and Swiss cheese au gratin. Crêpes Mixtes, two crêpes with scallops and mushrooms is flambéed with cognac in cream sauce. For those with other tastes, Patrice has concocted Timbales Neptune made up of scampis and shrimp in a pastry shell and Steak le Refuge, a T-bone with mushrooms flambéed with cognac and cream. A really unusual creation is Le Petit Lili — mushrooms stuffed with snails and garlic butter gratinéed with Swiss cheese. *Prices:* moderate.

Directions: Leave the Autoroute 10 at Exit #68 and proceed south on Route 139 for 40 kilometres (25 miles) past Cowansville to Sutton.

La Vieille Maison Eastman

Rue Des Pins
Eastman, Québec
J0E 1P0

Innkeepers: Marlene and Jean-Claude Rousseau
Telephone: 514-297-2288
Credit Cards: All major cards
Facilities: Dining. Fully licensed. Open year-round, Tuesday to Sunday.

Back in the 1890s, La Vieille Maison was the residence of the manager of a copper-mine complex. Actually, it was a *domaine* in the sense that there were two residences on the property. The other one was that of the groundskeeper. Many of Jean-Claude's older male guests say that they used to love to come out to the mine manager's homestead on any pretext just to catch a glimpse of his extremely attractive daughter.

Marlene and Jean-Claude bought the house in 1978 and completely refurbished it, being extremely careful to retain the grace and charm of this old Victorian home set in the pines of the Eastern Townships. Guests may sit out on the verandah or patio, weather permitting, and revel in the scenery while sipping an aperitif. However, the real business at hand is to make your selections from a fine menu fashioned by Marlene and Jean-Claude. Jean-Claude suggests a light snow-crabmeat mousse at $3.25 to "whet your appetite".

A chef whose meals have been celebrated in the *Montreal Calendar Magazine*, Jean-Claude also recommends jumbo shrimps in creole sauce à la Antoine, or Escalope of Veal in a cream sauce with mushrooms. There is so much summer theatre in the area that La Vieille Maison offers before-theatre specials of table d'hôte dinners of scampis or porterhouse steak. *Prices:* moderate.

Also, there are pastas on the menu, such as Fettucini Alfredo with cream and cheese sauce or the traditional frog's legs sautéed "à ma façon" as Jean-Claude phrases it.

Directions: Eastman is 94 kilometres (58 miles) east of Montreal, just off Autoroute 10 at Exit #106.

Le Château du Lac

85, rue Merry
Magog, Québec
J1X 3L2

Innkeeper: Jean-Claude Milot
Telephone: 819-843-2921
Credit Cards: MasterCard, Visa
Facilities: Dining. Open daily year-round. Fully licensed.

This lovely old Victorian château overlooking the Magog River was once the home and office of beloved old "Doc" Bowman. Here, he practised medicine and conducted his clinics. Either he profited very well from his practice or had little faith in the security of the banks because he kept a huge safe in the front room that remains there to this day.

All of the graceful features of this mansion have been retained by Jean-Claude, including a charming sitting room he has set aside overlooking the river, as an oasis for afternoon teas or late night coffee and liqueurs.

Le Château has a simple à la carte menu. Jean-Claude tells me the favourites are Truite meunière, Côtelettes de porc, and Brochette de Filet Mignon. Other selections include a slice of grilled salmon, filet of sole amandine and various other brochettes — chicken, ham, pork and seafood. *Prices:* inexpensive.

Directions: Magog is just off Autoroute 10, 120 kilometres (75 miles) east of Montreal.

Le Gosier

145, rue Michaud
Coaticook, Québec
J1A 1A9

Innkeeper: Donald Brunelle
Telephone: 819-849-4949
Credit Cards: MasterCard, Visa,
American Express
Facilities: Open daily year-round.
Fully licensed. Dinner: 5-10 p.m.
Sunday Brunch: 1-2 p.m.

It's hard to know where to start in describing Le Gosier and Coaticook. Coaticook, less than 7 kilometres from the U.S. border, has achieved success through a civic effort to make the most of what nature has provided.

The Coaticook gorge is a geological phenomenon caused by years of water erosion from the Coaticook River. This erosion has laid bare the geological history of the area over eons of time. To view this in the caves and gorge in the park is fascinating. The Société de Développement has preserved and promoted this as a tourist attraction and has done it quite successfully.

The same action of the river that caused the unusual geological formations made it possible to put up a small hydro plant and textile plant. As a result, the Penmans plant and warehouse were built in Coaticook over 100 years ago. In 1968, the Société bought the warehouse, and three years later Don and his wife, Irene, leased the building to create a beautiful restaurant.

The Brunelles have enhanced the brick interior and restored the original beams and columns of the warehouse. They even kept the forge which is now used during the fall and winter as a huge fireplace and spit, complete with racks for barbecuing whole boars — sounds like a medieval feast!

I asked Don why his logo was that of a long neck goose. "Le Gosier is the long throat of the goose which signifies the gorge," he replied.

For dinner, Don suggested that I try the Coeur de mignon le Gosier. I cannot recall eating a more tender, delicious steak. It was flambéed in Courvoisier, at the table, and served with a delicious herb sauce. Other items on the à la carte menu include a 7 seas platter (seafood for two), Chateaubriand bouquetière for two, and Brochette of scallops, oriental style. Full-course meals include Filet of turbot italienne, marinated Brochette of lamb and seafood on the half-shell. *Prices:* moderate-to-expensive.

During the summer, the theatre bar next door has performances by a local company.

Directions: Proceed south from Sherbrooke 8 kilometres (5 miles) to Route 147. Continue south on Route 147 approximately 27 kilometres (17 miles) to Coaticook.

Le GOSIER

Menu à la carte

Le Loft

Route 139
West Brome, Québec
J0E 2P0

Innkeeper: Rob Newcombe
Telephone: 514-263-3294
Rooms: 11 (shared baths)
Rates: very inexpensive
Credit Cards: MasterCard, Visa,
American Express
Facilities: Dining, tennis, heated
swimming pool, hot tub, sauna,
riding, hayrides. Golf, alpine and
cross-country skiing nearby in the
famous Sutton-Orford skiing
country. Fully licensed. Open
year-round.

Rob introduced me to one of his guests, a spritely Cécile Darbé, of United Empire Loyalist stock, who has a keen memory for local history. She explained that the farm where Le Loft is located, was first settled by Adrian Bisaillon over a hundred years ago. The original farmhouse has been refurbished and extended over the years. Rob, a ski buff himself, created a simple and inexpensive way for families to enjoy the magnificent Quebec countryside year-round. He evolved the idea of Le Loft as a club where families can bunk in together while enjoying all of the many facilities on site and in the surrounding area. Rob tells me that he is well advanced and plans to create ten condominium units ready for occupancy in the fall of 1984.

I dropped into Le Loft for Sunday brunch which included tourtière, beef, chicken wings with fried rice, ham, and garlic spareribs. For dessert, doughnuts, pastry and fresh fruit filled out the menu.

Rob calls his menu "The Feed Bag" and that is what you get — a plain kraft shopping bag with selections printed on it. While talking to Rob, I looked out on the lawn and noticed a rather devilish-looking contraption. Rob told me that it was a barbecue spit where, every Friday and Saturday, he barbecues a whole hind-quarter of beef. Other items on the menu include Pork Ribs, Beef Brochette, Sunday Scallops and the famous Lac-Brôme duckling. Prices: moderate.

Directions: Leave Autoroute 10 at Exit #68 and proceed south on Route 139, 30 kilometres (18 miles) to West Brome.

Les Trois Marmites

475 ouest, rue Principale
Magog, Québec
J1X 2B2

Innkeeper: Pierre Landreville
Telephone: 819-843-4448
Credit Cards: MasterCard, Visa,
American Express
Facilities: Dining. Fully licensed.
Open daily year-round.

I had lunch with Pierre and learned that Les Trois Marmites began in 1883 as a general store. In the oldest section of the building, Pierre found a well that originally was part of the water supply system for part of Magog.

The choice of the name Les Trois Marmites — The Three Cauldrons — is Pierre's way of telling everyone that his customers' favourite foods are chicken, beef and fish. The items on the menu that find the greatest favour are two table d'hôte selections: roast beef with a choice of potatoes, and asparagus tips, soup, dessert, coffee and a carafe of wine; the other popular item is broiled scampis with a starter of breaded St-Benoît cheese, from the nearby monastery, with dessert, coffee and a carafe of wine. Other items include veal scallopini Normand served on a bed of rice, baby clams in a garlic sauce served on spaghettini and crabmeat salad. *Prices:* moderate.

Pierre emphasizes that Les Trois Marmites is "a fine family restaurant for discerning travellers". He pointed out that he makes sure his wine list is kept as inexpensive as possible to cater to the large family trade he enjoys.

Directions: Magog is just off Autoroute 10, 120 kilometres (75 miles) east of Montreal.

Dans un accueil qui prédispose
intimate, cozy and inviting

L'Oeuf

229, Chemin Mystic
Mystic, Québec
J0J 1Y0

Innkeeper: Pierre Normandeau
Telephone: 514-248-7529
Credit Cards: No cards
Facilities: Dining. Open year-round, Sunday to Wednesday.
Lunch: 11:30 a.m. - 2 p.m. Dinner:
5 - 11:30 p.m.

The building which houses L'Oeuf has two sections. One end contains the former small grocery store which still bears the old Salada Tea window imprints. Next door is the current Crêperie.

Pierre Foglia, of Montreal's *La Presse*, claims to have given up on crêpes because they always turned out tough and leathery. Pierre Normandeau's creations, however, are soft and tender and very popular — all 67 of them!

Pierre's parents sat and talked with me while their son prepared and served his delicious crêpes. His father, dressed in leather alpine shorts, told me that he was recently retired from the Canadian customs service in which he had been attached to the Canadian Forces in the Black Forest, Germany. Madame Normandeau showed me a bread she had fashioned, in the shape of two chickens and a huge egg, in celebration of l'Oeuf's fifth anniversary. It sat on a near-by shelf, preserved in egg white.

In 1867, this building was first constructed as a general store and

post office. During the next 100 years, the building was expanded to provide a family residence for the storekeepers. (In its centennial year, the post office was closed.)

Pierre serves regular and fruit crêpes. The favourite is the Crêpe Maison containing ham, cheese, peas, potatoes, onions and mushrooms. *Prices:* inexpensive.

Directions: From Autoroute 10, take Exit #48 and proceed south, on Route 233 and 104, 12 kilometres (7 miles) to Route 235. Continue south 13 kilometres (8 miles) to Mystic.

❖❖❖❖❖❖❖❖❖❖❖❖❖❖❖❖❖❖❖❖❖❖❖❖❖❖❖❖❖❖

Manoir des Érables

220, rue du Manoir
Montmagny, Québec
G5V 1G5

Innkeepers: Renaud and Lorraine Cyr
Telephone: 418-248-0100
Rooms: 21 (all with bath)
Rates: moderate
Credit Cards: MasterCard, Visa, American Express
Facilities: Dining. Outdoor pool, golf nearby. Open March 21 to December 19.

We dropped into the Manoir for lunch and met both Renaud and Lorraine. Over a simple but delicious meal, Renaud talked of his two obsessions. The most pressing at that moment was the restoration of the upper floors and seven rooms of his inn, which had been badly damaged in a recent fire. Showing us through the devastated area, he spoke as if he had lost a member of his family. An integral part of the home that had existed for over 300 years had been destroyed and he felt it as a deep personal loss.

However, it was a different person who talked with animated passion about his vocation, the preparation of food. His firm conviction is that the people of Quebec must change their attitude about their traditional foods, such as pork and rabbit. With considerable force, he declared "We must take the traditional Quebec dishes and update them with new recipes." Not exactly "Nouvelle Cuisine", I think, but perhaps a "Nouvelle Cuisine Québécoise".

That he should want to forge firm lines between the past and the present comes as no surprise. He is the owner of a residence whose history stretches back 350 years. Louis Couillard de l'Espinay, the first seigneur of the area, built this mansion in 1655. Destroyed by invading English armies in 1759 and rebuilt some 50 years later, it survived several changes of ownership until it became an inn in 1953. Built mostly of local stone, the front of the house is graced with an open verandah and patio which offer delightful dining in the summer.

The dining room itself is furnished in gracious turn-of-the-century style with beautiful chandeliers, antique furniture and lace table-cloths. It was here that we were treated to a meal worthy of the Manoir's inclusion in the prestigious *Relais et Châteaux de France.*

Our waitress, resplendent in an evening gown, carefully and lovingly described our choices: smoked St. Lawrence sturgeon with lemon, rabbit liver pâté and shrimps à la Provençale, to name only a couple. The salad bar, filled with fresh vegetables bathed in herbs and seasonings, was a special delight. The French-Canadian pea soup was light and delicate to the taste. I enjoyed the cod tongues, an unusual and savoury dish and a perfect example of Renaud's intention of creating new Quebec dishes. It is not hard to understand why Renaud has been chosen as a member of Canada's national culinary team for the 1984 World Food Olympics to be held in Frankfurt.

For dessert we both ordered fruit salad: oranges, grapes, blue-berries, kiwi, all indescribably flavoured. The evening turned into a bit of a celebration as Renaud announced that his restoration plans could proceed because the government had agreed to support his project. *Prices: expensive.*

Directions: Montmagny is 70 kilometres (43 miles) east of Quebec City on Autoroute 20.

Manoir Hovey

Route Magog
North Hatley, Québec
J0B 2C0

Innkeepers: Kathryn and Stephen Stafford
Telephone: 819-842-2421
Rooms: 29 (all with bath)
Rates: (M.A.P.) moderate
Credit Cards: MasterCard, Visa, American Express
Facilities: Dining. Fully licensed. Tennis, boating, water skiing, cross-country skiing, beach.

As I walked into the reception foyer of the Manoir Hovey, I noticed a large 18th-Century Quebec armoire. Atop this armoire sat a celebrated 80-day Gothic-style clock that is rumoured to be haunted. As local legend has it, Plumley Lebaron, who had taken to wearing raccoon coats in the summer, haunts the clock and causes it to chime, but only if you mention his name. Suffice it to say that I never even breathed his name.

Around the turn of the century, a wealthy American southerner, Henry Atkinson, President of Georgia Power of Atlanta, built a magnificent summer home on Lake Massawippi. He built what

became almost an exact replica of George Washington's home at Mount Vernon, Virginia. From the lake, one can see the magnificent columns supporting the second-floor porch and the lovely white clapboard frame building. Atkinson was such an admirer of Washington that an original portrait of him painted on glass hangs in the dining room.

Steve Stafford took me on a tour of his domain. His imagination and ingenuity is really amazing. He has converted the servants' quarters, icehouse, pumphouse and electrical house into guest cottages, each furnished with genuine Canadian antiques. A special treat for me was the Coach House with its huge doors. The Coach House has been put to good use as a tavern where, every Saturday, the chef barbecues steak, salmon and lobster for guests at the Manoir.

Each one of the twenty-nine rooms is uniquely decorated with authentic antiques; nine of the rooms have wood-burning fireplaces. In the fall and winter, continuous supplies of wood are brought to the guests' rooms to provide a cheery glow to ward off the chill.

The dining room is more formal and the food lives up to the reputation of the inn. The featured items on the menu include the famous Lac-Brôme duck, sautéed veal sweetbreads and fresh Gaspé salmon. Other items are medallions of pork tenderloin with port and kiwi, assorted seafoods in white wine sauce on the half-shell, grilled sirloin steak and supreme of chicken with raspberry vinegar. Prices: moderate.

Directions: From Autoroute 10, take Exit #121 to Route 55. Proceed south 16 kilometres (10 miles) to Exit #29 and take Route 108 east 12 kilometres (7 miles) to North Hatley.

⚜⚜⚜⚜⚜⚜⚜⚜⚜⚜⚜⚜⚜⚜⚜⚜⚜⚜⚜⚜⚜⚜

Restaurant La Chapelle

5209, rue Frontenac
Lac-Mégantic, Québec
G6B 1H2

Innkeeper: Serge Parent
Telephone: 819-583-2125
Credit Cards: MasterCard, Visa, American Express
Facilities: Dining. Open daily year-round. Fully licensed. Lunch: 11 a.m. - 2 p.m. Dinner: 5-9 p.m.

In most of the towns I have visited, it is quite common to find someone who knows the history of the town and its buildings quite well.

In Lac-Mégantic, the history buff I tracked down was a very young woman, Françoise Giroux Marchand.

Françoise explained that La Chapelle's site had a triple history. The first English school was built here before the turn of the century and was maintained by the English School Commission. Around 1908, the Commission sold the site to St. Andrew's Presbyterian Church. At that time, there was quite a flourishing population of Presbyterians in Lac-Mégantic. However, as time passed, this population declined and finally, in 1977, the building was sold to Serge Parent and his partners, who set out to provide first-class dining while maintaining the integrity of this historic building.

Both the exterior and the interior remain faithful to its religious origin. Even the clothes hooks in the vestibule have been kept. Upstairs, in the choir loft, the armchairs and church benches supply the seating. The beautiful stained glass windows imported from France lend a warmth and charm to the atmosphere of the restaurant. The brightly polished, original hardwood floors complete the picture.

Serge tells me that his favourite menu items, and that of his guests, are the Salmon with Brittany sauce, Lac-Brôme duckling for two, and the Brochette of Compton chicken. Filling out the menu is a wide range of dishes including filet mignon with mushrooms, filet mignon and scampis, pepper steak flambéed and steak tartare. Desserts include such Québécois staples as pears flambéed and cake with maple syrup. *Prices:* moderate.

Directions: From Sherbrooke, drive south on Route 143 a few kilometres to Lennoxville; turn east on Route 108, 71 kilometres (44 miles) to Stornoway. Then drive south on Route 161, 27 kilometres (16 miles) to Lac-Mégantic.

✦✦✦✦✦✦✦✦✦✦✦✦✦✦✦✦✦✦✦✦✦✦✦✦✦

The Townshipper

Main Street
Knowlton, Québec
J0E 1V0

Innkeepers: Christa and Milan Vavrousek
Telephone: 514-943-5439
Credit Cards: MasterCard, Visa
Facilities: Dining. Fully licensed. Open year-round. Summer: 11:30 a.m. - 9:30 p.m. Winter (Closed Mondays)

Christa and Milan first came to Canada from Czechoslovakia in 1968, the year of the Russian invasion, and in 1978 took over the operation of The Townshipper.

A 130-year-old house that was occupied by William Henry Drummond from 1896-1905, this restaurant's sailing motif comes from one

of his poems. Christa explained that one of his poems tells the story of some fishermen caught in the ice of a lake that suddenly froze over. Miraculously, it opened up and they returned safely to their families.

Christa and Milan specialize in mid-European food. The favourites are roast duckling, goulash, schnitzel and two pork dishes. All dishes are accompanied by bread dumplings and red cabbage. *Prices:* inexpensive.

Directions: Leave Autoroute 10 at Exit #90. Proceed south on Route 243, around Lac-Brôme for 12 kilometres (7 miles) to Knowlton.

Lower St. Lawrence & Gaspé

This area, on the south shore of the St. Lawrence, stretching from Quebec City around the Gaspé peninsula, reaches back into the maritime history of Quebec. Here, at Gaspé, a cross marks the landing of Jacques Cartier in 1534. In 1984, 450 years later, the event was commemorated by the sailing of the Tall Ships from St-Malo in France (Cartier's embarkation port) following his route to Gaspé and then down the St. Lawrence. Though the population is mostly of French origin, United Empire Loyalists, Irish and even Jersey Islanders have mixed their background in this fascinating area.

Of course, fishing plays a large part in the economy of the area as reflected in the menus of the inns and the flock of fishing boats in the various port towns.

The short drive from Gaspé to Percé is an experience never to be forgotten — one spectacular sight after another, topped off by the awe-inspiring Rock at Percé. At low tide I made a valiant attempt to walk out to the end of the rock but was turned back by slippery footing and a lack of fortitude.

Lower St. Lawrence and Gaspé

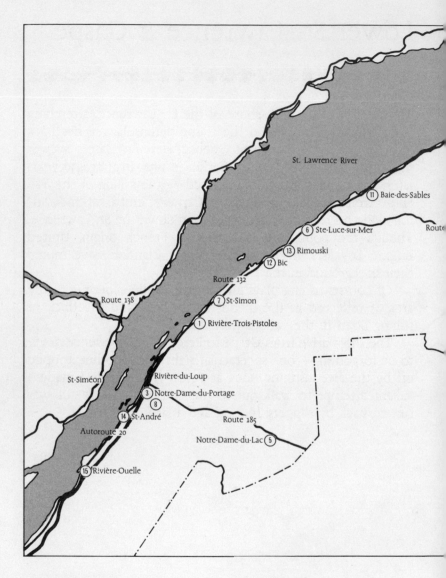

St. Lawrence River

⑪ Baie-des-Sables

Route

⑥ Ste-Luce-sur-Mer

⑬ Rimouski

⑫ Bic

Route 132

Route 138

⑦ St-Simon

① Rivière-Trois-Pistoles

St-Siméon

Rivière-du-Loup

③ Notre-Dame-du-Portage

⑧

⑭ St-André

Route 185

Autoroute 20

Notre-Dame-du-Lac ⑤

⑮ Rivière-Ouelle

1 Auberge de la Rivière	5 Auberge Marie Blanc
2 Auberge du Parc	6 Auberge Ste-Luce
3 Auberge du Portage	7 Auberge St-Simon
4 Auberge le Coin-du-Banc	8 Auberge sur Mer

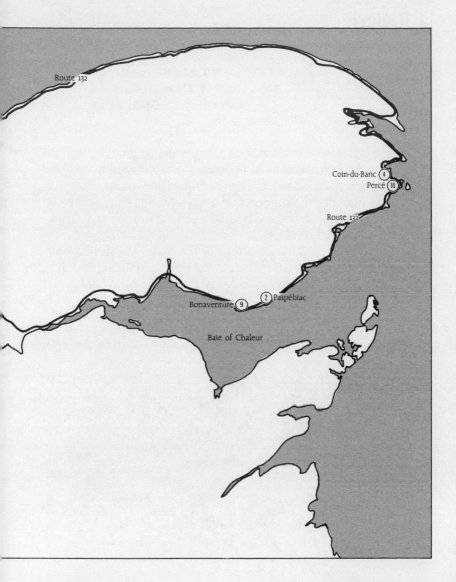

Route 132

Coin-du-Banc ④

Percé ⑩

Route 132

Bonaventure ⑨ ② Paspébiac

Baie of Chaleur

9   Café l'Indépendant
10 Hôtel Bleu Blanc Rouge
11 La Meunière
12 Le Vieux Manoir du Français

13 Maison Chez-Robert
14 Manoir St-André
15 Villa Fleur des Bois

Auberge de la Rivière

1, rue de la Grève
Rivière-Trois-Pistoles, Québec
GoL 2E0

Innkeeper: Mme Denis L. Rioux
Telephone: 418-851-9932
Rooms: 12; 1 with private bath,
11 share common washroom
Rates: very inexpensive
Credit Cards: No cards
Facilities: Dining, fishing,
snowshoeing. Open all year-
round.

Mme Rioux greeted me warmly as she has no doubt done for all other guests in her 27 years as an innkeeper. Her Auberge is a simple place, with nicely decorated and very comfortable rooms.

The inn was once the residence of a manager of Tobin Limitée, a forest products company. It also housed a general store to serve company employees and residents.

As Mme Rioux took me on a tour of the place, I noticed a very old and massive piano. I asked her how old it was and she replied that it was over a hundred years old and was in need of a tuning. I guess that after a hundred years a tuning might be in order!

Directions: Rivière-Trois-Pistoles is just 60 kilometres (37 miles) west of Rimouski on Route 132.

Auberge du Parc

68, boulevard Notre-Dame
Paspébiac, Québec
GoC 2Ko

Innkeepers: M. and Mme A. Lemarquand
Telephone: 418-752-3355
Rooms: 11 (3 with bath) in the Auberge; 25 motel units with bath
Rates: very inexpensive-to-expensive
Credit Cards: MasterCard, Visa
Facilities: Dining. Open May to October.

Those who travel through Quebec and the Maritimes are familiar with the small chain of department stores called Robin Jones and Whitman. The guiding genius of this chain was the very enterprising Charles Robin, a native of the Jersey Islands. The folk of these British Islands found their way to North America where Robin became a fish merchant, processing and exporting, and later a general merchant with many stores. His fish-processing plant, located on the shore and once destroyed by fire, has been restored and declared an historical monument by the Quebec government. The former warehouse for the chain is located right next door to the inn.

Robin preferred to settle in his native Islands, but he did build a palatial home for the general manager of his Canadian operations. Dating back to 1880 and situated on a forested slope overlooking the Baie des Chaleurs, the current magnificent Victorian home has been lovingly maintained in all its grace and charm by the Lemarquands. The old sunporch has been enclosed to provide a complete dining room. The luxurious gardens have also been impeccably kept and remain intact to provide many of the fruits and vegetables used in the kitchen.

Mme Lemarquand very graciously offered me a drink and as I was enjoying it she described the highlights of her menu. The specialties centre around the sea — sole, lamb and shrimps, plus a Coquille de fruits de mer au gratin and a rather unusual eight-ounce salmon stuffed with small shrimps. *Prices:* moderate.

Directions: Paspébiac is approximately 100 kilometres (62 miles) west of Percé on Route 132.

❧❧❧❧❧❧❧❧❧❧❧❧❧❧❧❧❧❧❧❧❧❧❧❧❧

Auberge du Portage

671 Route du Fleuve
Notre-Dame-du-Portage, Québec
G0L 1Y0

Innkeepers: Claude and Ginette De Foy
Telephone: 418-862-3601
Rooms: 42 (all with bath)
Rates: very inexpensive
Credit Cards: MasterCard, Visa
Facilities: Dining, swimming pool, sauna, whirlpool. Fully licensed. Open June 1 to September 15.

The De Foys, who have owned the Auberge du Portage since 1970, have published a little pamphlet about their establishment. Rather fittingly, it begins by welcoming guests in the name of all members of the family — Ginette, Claude, Caroline and Alexandre.

The origins of the inn go back to 1892 when Napoléon Boulay, of nearby Rivière-du-Loup, sold the property as a summer residence to August Robert, a lumber merchant from Montreal who built a gracious turn-of-the-century manor with many towers and balconies. In 1911, Madame Joseph Eugène Pelletier, along with her sons, added a three-storey building and called it The Portage Inn.

Ginette and Claude bought the inn in 1970 and have succeeded in providing the utmost in comfort while maintaining the inn's charms and ambience. Many items of furniture in the lobby are original 19th-Century pieces.

The table d'hôte menu reflects the simple fare of the St. Lawrence shore: filet of cod, roast pork and salmon pâté. *Prices:* inexpensive.

Directions: Notre-Dame-du-Portage is just a few kilometres west of Rivière-du-Loup, or 200 kilometres (124 miles) east of Quebec City on Route 132. Also accessible from Autoroute 20.

❦❦❦❦❦❦❦❦❦❦❦❦❦❦❦❦❦❦❦❦❦❦❦❦❦

Auberge le Coin-du-Banc

Route 132
Coin-du-Banc, Québec
GoC 2Lo

Innkeeper: Sidney Maloney
Telephone: 418-645-2907
Rooms: 9 (3 with bath, 6 with shared bath) in Auberge; 4 chalets with bath
Rates: moderate-to-expensive
Credit Cards: No cards
Facilities: Dining, sailing school, beach swimming, agate hunting. Open May through September; by reservation only from October through April.

As you enter the Auberge, a small welcome sign greets you in three languages — French, English and Gaelic. This sign is testament to the mixed heritage of this seafaring area and to the Irish ancestry of the current owner, Sidney Maloney.

The original French Settlers were from Normandy. Then, French-Protestant Huguenot families, who fled their native land to avoid persecution, arrived via the American colonies during the 1770s. They came as United Empire Loyalists and settled the area alongside Irish farmers who later left Ireland during the potato famine and were shipwrecked off the coast. Sometime later, Jersey Islanders from Britain arrived in search of the rich fishing grounds off the Gaspé peninsula and took up residence as the last large settlement group.

The former owners of the Auberge, the Mabé family, are descendants of the Huguenot Loyalists who found prosperity in the forest, farms and sea of Coin-du-Banc.

Sidney bought the house with its various additions in 1972. Built in the 1860s, the main house is furnished à la Gaspésienne: a random mixture of pieces inscribed with the fleur-de-lis or shamrock, reflecting their cultural origin. The *neigerie* or icehouse, used for freezing salmon for export, and the "stage", where fishing equipment was stored, have been converted into charming seaside "saltbox chalets" and they are much in demand.

The inn is frequented now by artists and writers who are beguiled by the inn's ambience and particularly its two main characters, Lise and Sid.

I arrived there for lunch and was served a simple but delicious meal of homemade bread, vegetable soup and a fluffy cheese omelette and finished off with hot apple pie. The dinner menu features seafood typical of the Gaspé area: Cod Tongue Intrigue (cooked in butter, cognac and orange peel); Morue à la Gaspésienne (poached cod topped with small pieces of fried salt pork); Gaspé lobster, salmon, scallops and halibut. Meat lovers will find pork, ham and T-bone steak. *Prices:* moderate.

Directions: Coin-du-Banc is 70 kilometres (43 miles) west of Gaspé on Route 132.

❧❧❧❧❧❧❧❧❧❧❧❧❧❧❧❧❧❧❧❧❧❧❧❧

Auberge Marie Blanc

1112, rue Commerciale
Notre-Dame-du-Lac, Québec

Innkeeper: Guy Sirois
Telephone: 418-899-6747
Rooms: 14 motel units with bath; 1 chalet
Rates: very inexpensive
Credit Cards: MasterCard, Visa
Facilities: Dining, swimming in Lac-Témiscouata, marina. Open from Easter to January.

One afternoon, we were sitting before the magnificent fireplace in what was the living room of the former Gray Lodge, when Guy Sirois's fourteen-year-old daughter came bursting into the room, just home from school. Her father, with a twinkle in his eye, asked her to tell the story of Marie Blanc. It seems that, in 1905 a New York lawyer named Bishop built this lovely home (reportedly designed by Frank Lloyd Wright) for his mistress, Marie Blanc Charlier. Originally from Martinique, she was the governess for his children and remained there with them all summer, while spending her winters in Nice.

We sat entranced as this lovely child innocently recounted the story of this lady who was the mistress of Mr. Bishop. To hear her talking, it sounded like a fairy story rather than something one keeps under wraps.

What is now a two-storey family chalet was the garage with the chauffeur's quarters upstairs. Guy tells me that a corduroy driveway was built to help the car ascend the steep incline of the road.

This family operation offers a Québécois cuisine using local geese, quail, lamb, rabbit and corégone (a local fish from Lac-Témiscouata).

Directions: From Québec City, take Autoroute 20 or scenic Route 132 approximately 140 kilometres (87 miles) past Notre-Dame-du-Portage. Then turn south on Route 185 for 50 kilometres (31 miles) to Notre-Dame-du-Lac.

❧❧❧❧❧❧❧❧❧❧❧❧❧❧❧❧❧❧❧❧❧❧❧❧❧❧❧❧❧❧❧

Auberge Ste-Luce

Ste-Luce-sur-Mer, Québec
G0K 1P0

Innkeeper: Roland Pigeon
Telephone: 418-738-4955
Rooms: 40; 25 with bath
Rates: very inexpensive
Credit Cards: MasterCard, Visa, Carte Blanche, Diner's Club
Facilities: Dining, beach swimming and boating. Open end of May to Labour Day.

Built in the early 19th Century by Hilari Jouvin, master pilot on the St. Lawrence, the original house remained in the hands of Jouvin relatives for over 100 years.

In 1949, a Mr. DeGagné, who operated the New Wellington Hotel in Sherbrooke, bought the home and refurbished it, turning it into an inn. Later, he added motel units which stretch back towards the St. Lawrence shore.

The menu reflects the maritime background of the owners and the area: Seafood fondue, Captain's plate of salmon, lobster, cod, shrimp and scallops, as well as other 'fruits of the sea'. *Prices:* inexpensive.

Directions: Ste-Luce-sur-Mer is a small village 2 kilometres (8 miles) east of Rimouski on Route 132.

Auberge St-Simon

18, rue Principale
St-Simon, Québec
G0L 4C0

Innkeepers: Frances Bélanger, Alain Choinière
Telephone: 418-738-2971
Rooms: 11; 6 with sink, 5 with bath
Rates: very inexpensive
Credit Cards: No cards
Facilities: Dining. Open May 15 to September 15.

Built in 1830, the inn was the home of the Bernier family until 1924. Marcel Bernier, the last member of the family to occupy the building, told me that it then became a general store-cum-residence until 1926 when it became an inn. In 1977, the Berniers sold it to Frances and Alain who have continued its operation.

It is a three-storeyed, Victorian-style building with a short, square roof and dormer windows. Although it is a simple country inn, its dinner menu is sophisticated and varied. One can have a choice of lamb, ragout of sturgeon, rabbit with prunes, and Gaspé lobster. *Prices:* inexpensive.

Directions: St-Simon is a small village 50 kilometres (31 miles) west of Rimouski.

Auberge sur Mer

363, Route du Fleuve
Notre-Dame-du-Portage, Québec
GoL 1Yo

Innkeepers: Mado and Jean April
Telephone: 418-862-3636
Rooms: 51
Rates: very inexpensive
Credit Cards: MasterCard, Visa
Facilities: Dining, swimming.
Auberge open May to October;
motel open year-round.

In April 1982, the local newspaper honoured Jean with an article headed "Jean April, The Innkeeper of Tradition". Upon reading it, one learns that the inn was built in 1890 by a Mr. Labbé. Jean's father, Ovide, purchased it over 75 years ago and passed it on to his son and grandchildren. Two of them, Annie and Elaine, are already studying at the famous Institut de Tourisme et Hôtelerie in Montreal.

While touring the inn, Jean showed me a collection of three hundred and seventy-five salt and pepper shakers that he purchased for a few thousand dollars. The collection is over 80 years old and includes shakers of every description, including fire trucks and animals. He welcomes questions from his guests on the unusual collection. Jean also obtained a hundred-year-old organ and clock, both of which work perfectly. Many evenings are spent around the organ with guests joining in the singing.

The rooms are well appointed and comfortable, and the motel units are situated close to the shore.

The table d'hôte menu features fresh seafood: cod, sole, salmon and smelts, as well as ham, steak and pork. *Prices:* inexpensive-to-moderate.

Directions: Notre-Dame-du-Portage is just a few kilometres west of Rivière-du-Loup, or 200 kilometres (124 miles) east of Quebec City on the picturesque Route 132. Also accessible from Autoroute 20.

Café l'Indépendant

C.P. 600
Rue du Quai
Carleton-sur-Mer, Bonaventure
Québec GoC 1Jo

Innkeeper: Pierre Landry
Telephone: 418-364-7602
Credit Cards: No cards
Facilities: Dining. Fully licensed.
Open daily (7 a.m. - 11 p.m.)

Narcisse le Blanc built this house in 1835 as his residence and place of business. At a mere 150 years old, it is reputed to be one of the oldest places in Carleton, while inns near Quebec City and along the St. Lawrence boast a three-hundred-year history. This sheds some light on the pattern of development in early Quebec. Settlements were concentrated along the St. Lawrence where shipping and transportation were most accessible. Settlements inland developed more slowly as people moved away from main commercial centres to establish new ventures in undeveloped areas.

Narcisse lived on, and operated a forge here for fifty or sixty years, after which it became a summer home, until Pierre bought it in 1977. When asked the significance of the name *l'Indépendant*, Pierre explained that it was chosen to personify his thrust for personal independence. Not unlike the early settlers in the area, he wanted to be his own man.

Café l'Indépendant is a simple clapboard building overlooking the Baie des Chaleurs. Pierre has enclosed a verandah and added onto the building to make it a viable restaurant. While I was eating, he made continuous trips to the open firewood stove that graced the dining area and provided welcome warmth to ward off the chill of a cold, rainy, early October evening.

In the frontispiece of his menu, Pierre states his culinary credo, "We have no culinary pretensions but since always having eaten well at mother's table, we are confident in serving you a good meal."

I put myself in his hands and was served the table d'hôte meal of a delicious onion soup with a main course of scallops in garlic sauce with mushrooms and cucumbers and a dessert of bread pudding with heavy cream and fresh strawberries. Other items on the menu include Croûte au crevettes ou crabes — shrimp or crab served in a fresh slice of French bread, and filet of cod or sole. *Prices:* moderate.

Directions: Carleton-sur-Mer is 200 kilometres (124 miles) west of Gaspé on Route 132.

Hôtel Bleu Blanc Rouge

104, Route 132
Percé, Québec
GoC 2Lo

Innkeepers: Pierre and Marie Bélanger
Telephone: 418-782-2142
Rooms: 7 (3 with bath) in the Auberge; 6 chalets with bath; 14 motel units on shore
Rates: very inexpensive-to-expensive
Credit Cards: MasterCard, Visa
Facilities: Dining, beach swimming, kitchenettes available. Open year-round.

As I was touring the Inn, I came upon a striking photograph of a man fashioning a fishing fly. It turned out to be a family snapshot of Marie Bélanger's father, Harry. He was pictured in his retirement pursuing a hobby that was intimately related to his original occupation — that of the traditional Gaspé fisherman. Every summer day long before sunrise, he would go to sea with his own boat, harvest his day's catch and return long after dark. In the winter, he would travel ten miles through the bitter cold into the backwoods to cut lumber for the local sawmill. Such was the traditional pattern of life in the Gaspé.

In an attempt to break from this pattern, the Bélangers built a house in 1920 and began to take in guests. As they prospered, they

Motel-Hôtel Bleu Blanc Rouge   Percé, Quebec

added rooms, chalets and eventually the motel. As Pierre explained to me, they expanded slowly but surely, financing the entire process from the profits and supplying their own hard labour. Even the table-cloths, curtains and chaircovers were handmade by Marie's mother and what works of art they were!

The hotel name, *Bleu Blanc Rouge*, was also chosen by Marie's mother who wanted a contrast to the English names of the other tourist homes in the area. The colours also honour the homeland of Jacques Cartier who discovered the Gaspé some 400 years ago in 1534. Pierre made a point of showing me the hand pump in the kitchen that still supplies all the drinking water for the dining rooms. It came from the area courthouse built before 1900.

The Bélangers have their own vegetable garden and make their own delicious bread and pastries. Madame Bélanger invited me for lunch. Having partaken of the lavish lunches that seem to be the custom in the country inns of Québec, I pleaded for a light repast and was served generous slices of homemade bread, delicious pea soup, cod gratiné and maple sugar pie. I didn't dare ask for a full meal!

The dinner menu features Bouillabaisse à la St-Pierre, a seafood soup with cod, sole, halibut, lobster and shrimps. There is also seafood gratinée with scallops, lobster, shrimp and crabs. Non-fish eaters can choose from roast beef or a salt-pork omelette. *Prices:* moderate.

Directions: Percé is 70 kilometres (43 miles) west of Gaspé on Route 132.

La Meunière

202, Route 132
Baie-des-Sables, Québec
J0T 1C0

Innkeeper: Marius Caron
Telephone: 418-772-6808
Credit Cards: MasterCard, Visa, American Express
Facilities: Dining. Open daily May to October. Lunch: 11 a.m. - 2 p.m.; dinner 6-10 p.m. Fully licensed.

This charming summer restaurant was originally a flour mill estab-lished in the early 19th Century by the Roy-Desjardins family. I met with the last owners of the mill, Robert and Angèle Roy, both hearty 80-year-olds who recounted the mill's history.

Their family traces its roots back to 1665 to the famous Carignan Regiment which had its base near Montreal. By 1838, the family had settled in Baie-des-Sables and built a sawmill as well as a flour mill, thus harnessing the power of the Page River. The millwheel was 26 feet in diameter and used four grinding stones which are now on the front lawn as a commemoration of the mill's past. The mill remained in operation under the direction of the Roy family until its closure in 1952. Some twenty years later, it was purchased by Marius who converted it into the current restaurant.

Two features of the restaurant celebrate its past. One is a wall of photographs of the Roy family going back to 1838. The other artifact is a flour mixer that stretches the length of the dining area. It is an imposing and attractive example of maple construction.

Marius indicated that the favourite menu items were l'Entrecôte du moulin, pepper steak flambé in cognac and, of course, the famous Matane Shrimps. Other Gaspé favourites include cod, salmon and crab plates. *Prices:* moderate.

Directions: Baie-des-Sables is about 70 kilometres (43 miles) east of Rimouski on Route 132.

❖❖❖❖❖❖❖❖❖❖❖❖❖❖❖❖❖❖❖❖❖❖❖❖❖

Le Vieux Manoir du Français
Route 132
Bic, Québec
G0L 1B0

Innkeeper: Gilbert Ouellet
Telephone: 418-736-4345
Rooms: 12; 2 with bath, 10 share common washroom
Rates: very inexpensive
Credit Cards: MasterCard, Visa, American Express
Facilities: Dining. Open year-round. Closed access to Le parc du Bic and summer theatre, fishing and boat excursions.

Though the history of Le Vieux Manoir goes back more than 100 years, today it is a beautiful, grandly furnished, small country inn owned by the Quebec Government. The reason for this is quite interesting. Over a hundred years ago, a building of unknown origin existed here. In 1937, Pierre Beaudry, of France, built a small inn which subsequently went through a number of hands and eventually began to deteriorate.

In the mid-1960s, the Quebec Government responded to a plea for employment in the area, whose economic situation had been chronically weak. It created a tourist attraction in Le parc du Bic. The only accommodation nearby was the run-down manoir, open only for a few months of the year. The government stepped in, bought and completely refurbished the place, cost being no object. As an example, a ventilation fan big enough to serve the largest kitchens was installed at a cost of $26 000. So powerful is it that, in the winter, its draft threatens to extinguish the fires in the fireplaces in the living and dining room areas. Other fans had to be installed to offset this effect.

The inn is now operated, under contract, by Gilbert Ouellet and partner Robert Carrier, who have succeeded in creating inviting surroundings and a fine cuisine.

I stopped by for dinner. Starting off with an entrée of scallops sautéed à la Provençale, I followed with a delicious, thick onion soup. The main course was grilled rib steak in mustard sauce. Other favourites on the à la carte menu are surf 'n turf, cod, sole and Brochettes de Filet Mignon. *Price:* moderate.

Directions: Bic is just a few kilometres west of Rimouski, 300 kilometres (186 miles) east of Quebec City on Route 132.

Maison Chez-Robert

214, rue Belzile
Rimouski, Québec
G5L 3C3

Innkeepers: Pierre Bourbonnais and
and André Turcotte
Telephone: 418-724-2131
Rooms: 7 (all with bath)
Rates: very inexpensive
Credit Cards: MasterCard, Visa,
American Express
Facilities: Dining. Open year-round.

The Thursday night prior to the Thanksgiving weekend, I arrived at Chez-Robert in the midst of La Fête d'Automne. The whole city was celebrating with a variety of events, from agricultural and craft expositions to dune buggy races. The motto for the celebration, "Je Cousine et Toi?", translated roughly means "a gathering of the brotherhood." And what a gathering it was! For three days, Chez-Robert rocked with the festivities.

The most illustrious owner of this inn was Jules Brillant who lived here from 1923 until his death in 1977. He played an important role in the development of the region as the President of the Electric Company of Amqui, Québec Telephone and The Power Company of Bas St-Laurent, to name a few. He was also influential in establishing the Technical and Marine School of Rimouski and the School of Commerce.

Chez-Robert is a gracious 19th-Century manor house set back from the road. Its main floor has been converted to accommodate three dining areas and a very joyous bar. The lovely porch and terrace have been added to the back for enjoyable summer dining.

I was fortunate to have dinner there. Starting off with delicious Escargots de Bourgogne à la Provençale, I followed with the main course of lamb brochette served on a bed of rice with onion rings and green peppers. For dessert, I was served Profiterolles au chocolat — a type of chocolate éclair with ice cream smothered in chocolate sauce. Many regional dishes such as salmon, halibut, rabbit, steaks and surf 'n turf, fill out the menu. *Prices:* moderate.

Directions: Rimouski is 312 kilometres (194 miles) east of Quebec City on Route 132.

❈❈❈❈❈❈❈❈❈❈❈❈❈❈❈❈❈❈❈❈❈❈❈❈

Manoir St-André

Route 132
St-André, Québec
GoL 2Ho

Innkeepers: Emilie and Cécile Morel
Telephone: 418-493-2082
Rooms: 8 in Manoir (shared baths); 6 cabins, all with bath
Rates: very inexpensive
Credit Cards: MasterCard, Visa
Facilities: Dining. Open year-round.

St-André is a tiny village sitting on the St. Lawrence, and the Manoir is an elegant, small inn built in 1855 by the Marquis family. Painted white and Victorian in style, it is set off with green trim.

The inn remained in the family until 1955 when it was sold to a religious order for use as a school. In 1965, it became the country inn it is today. The Morels work extremely hard to provide the ambience for which the Quebec country inns are so famous.

Seafood is the specialty of the menu and includes salmon, kipper,

halibut, cod, and lobster. Entrées are served in ample portions and are absolutely delicious. *Prices:* very inexpensive.

Directions: St-André is a few miles west of Rivière-du-Loup, approximately 160 kilometres (100 miles) east of Quebec City on Route 132. It can also be reached by driving up Route 138 on the north shore and crossing the St. Lawrence by ferry at St-Siméon. The one and a half-hour ferry ride is a pleasant one and costs a minimum of $18.80.

Villa Fleur des Bois

Route au Quai
Rivière-Ouelle, Québec
G0L 2C0

Innkeeper: Gilles Lortie
Telephone: 418-856-1201
Rooms: 10
Rates: (A.P.) very inexpensive
Credit Cards: MasterCard, Visa
Facilities: Dining, outdoor heated swimming pool. Open June to September.

The Villa was originally built in 1917, in Lévis, for use as a hotel. When the municipal authorities expropriated it to make way for a road, the Chanoine (Canon) Lemieux, parish priest of Robertsonville, purchased it for his use as a residence.

However, because his residence was actually 113 kilometres away, the building was dismantled, each piece carefully numbered, and transported by boat to Rivière-Ouelle. He finally occupied the house in 1922.

The Canon received many prominent guests during his 32 years there, including cabinet ministers, monseigneurs, and Cardinal Villeneuve. The dining room, le Salon Cardinalice, was named in honour of one of his visits. The Chanoine died in 1956 and, in 1972, the building was returned to its original use as an inn.

The dining room, Le Chanoine, serves a wide selection of dinners including steaks, Gaspé lobster, local smelts and fondues. *Prices:* moderate.

Directions: Rivière-Ouelle is on Route 132, about 120 kilometres (74 miles) east of Quebec City.

Charlevoix

Driving along Route 138 from Quebec City to Tadoussac you will see perhaps the most stunningly beautiful country in Canada. The road — a fine highway — hugs the St. Lawrence shoreline. Within a few minutes one is either plunging down with a spectacular view of valley and shore or climbing steeply towards the sky. Little villages nestle in the valleys and the sunshine sparkles on the blue St. Lawrence. It is no wonder that there are many artists' colonies in Charlevoix, particularly in the Baie St-Paul and Pointe-au-Pic areas.

Though fur traders exploited the area in the 17th Century and later the timber barons, such as Price and Donohue, developed the forest resources, it wasn't until the latter part of the 19th Century that tourists discovered its grandeur. For some reason, what used to be called Murray Bay became the summer playground for wealthy Americans (including President Taft). Many of these grand homes have become excellent inns and have very interesting stories to tell.

The tourist establishments are dominated by the Manoir Richelieu — a grand hotel in the old tradition — with granite walls and a copper roof. Here and in the Bas St-Laurent area, more than anywhere in Quebec, one finds establishments that have been run by the same family over many generations. This represents the transition from farming to tourism.

Charlevoix

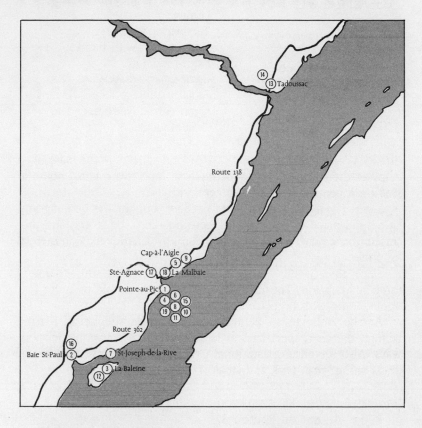

1	Auberge au Petit Berger	11	Auberge les Sources
2	Auberge Belle Plage	12	Hôtel Cap aux Pierres
3	Auberge de la Roche Pleureuse	13	Hôtel Georges
4	Auberge des Falaises	14	Hôtel Tadoussac
5	Auberge des Peupliers	15	La Maison Donohue
6	Auberge des Trois Canards	16	La Maison Otis
7	Auberge la Perdriole	17	Le Club des Monts
8	Auberge la Petite Marmite	18	Manoir Charlevoix
9	Auberge la Pinsonnière	19	Manoir Richelieu
10	Auberge la Rose au Bois		

Auberge au Petit Berger

1, Côte Bellevue
Pointe-au-Pic, Québec
GoT 1Mo

Innkeepers: Jacques and Marthe Lemire
Telephone: 418-665-4182
Rooms: 20 (10 with bath)
Rates: moderate
Credit Cards: MasterCard, Visa
Facilities: Dining. Tennis. Dining room closed November 1 to December 15.

Charles Warren, the architect whose name appears in the plans of so many of the summer homes in the area, built this original home in 1896 for a gentleman from California.

Later, Edgar Desbien, an area resident, bought the building as a home and place of business. In these buildings, he stored and processed the catches brought in to him by Charlevoix commercial fishermen.

Since 1979, Jacques and Marthe have operated this charming three-building inn. The rooms vary from very simple to quite luxurious, some with fireplace and whirlpool.

At the Auberge au Petit Berger (the little shepherd), Marthe Lemire, the chef, specializes in lamb presented in various delicious ways. Also served are traditional Quebec and Charlevoix dishes of duck, rabbit, veal, pork and steak. *Price:* expensive.

Directions: Pointe-au-Pic is 150 kilometres (93 miles) east of Quebec City on Route 362, just off Route 138.

Auberge Belle Plage

192, rue Ste-Anne
Baie St-Paul, Québec
CoA 1Bo

Innkeepers: Jeanne and Guy Mathieu
Telephone: 418-435-9921
Rooms: 17 auberge rooms (2 shared baths); 4 motel units (all with bath)
Rates: (M.A.P.) inexpensive
Credit Cards: MasterCard, Visa
Facilities: Dining, outdoor pool, and marina. Closed November.

While driving around the beautiful Baie St-Paul area, I was impressed with the number of artist's studios and shops. I found a pottery place on a small side road outside of Baie St-Paul. Because I was shopping I knocked at the door of the private home and was greeted by a charming lady. Standing there on her patio, I was treated to a stunning view of the river, shore and hills. I turned and said, "you know, you really don't deserve this." With a very sweet smile she replied, "Oh, I think we do." Whether they deserve it or not, the residents of this area are certainly blessed with magnificent scenery. Jeanne Mathieu showed me a document, a sort of lyric essay, on finding and falling in love with the area. As she wrote, "C'était le paradis! Quoi?" (Paradise it is, indeed.)

Auberge Belle Plage was built 130 years ago as the residence of the

local manager of the Abitibi paper mill. When the company left the area, the house remained closed for some time. Jeanne and Guy bought the home in 1977 and have turned it into a very simple and charming inn.

The table d'hôte menu, which varies each day, abounds with the specialties of the area: sole, rabbit, smelts, lamb and salmon. *Prices:* expensive.

Directions: Baie St-Paul is 80 kilometres (50 miles) east of Quebec City on Route 138.

Auberge de la Roche Pleureuse

238 est, Route Principale
La-Baleine, Île-aux-Coudres
Québec GoA 2Ao

Innkeeper: Rita Dufour Laurin
Telephone: 418-438-2232
Rooms: 81
Rates: moderate
Credit Cards: No cards
Facilities: Dining, tennis, outdoor pool. Open May 15 to October 15.

Madame Laurin received me in a quiet, direct way. Her ancestry goes back twelve generations to the 16th Century when the area was first settled. I succeeded in breaking down her reserve sufficiently for her to show me selections from a book by Edna Staebler, *What Happened to Maggie?* The story quotes Rita's grandmother Irma Dufour: "We couldn't pass over if we paid architek, so we planned it all ourself. My brodder made de dining room but like he make a bird-house, with the ceiling look like a church. We stain de pinewood and trim it with French Blue. Ain't it pretty? — When Mr. Saint Laurent, Prime Minister of Canada stay here, he say dey're very nice." Needless to say, Mr. Saint Laurent wasn't wrong. They are very nice.

This old family home, built in 1858, started in the guest business by taking in a few visitors. It has now expanded to include a motel. The table d'hôte menu, which changes daily, includes fresh St. Lawrence trout, poulet à l'érable, tourtière and roast smelts. Desserts include the traditional sugar tarts and pudding chômeur (bread pudding). *Prices:* moderate.

Directions: Île-aux-Coudres is a short ferry ride from St-Joseph-de-la-Rive, 110 kilometres (68 miles) east of Quebec City, off Route 362.

Auberge des Falaises

18, boulevard des Falaises
Pointe-au-Pic, Québec
GoT 1Mo

Innkeepers: Denys and Reine
Cloutier
Telephone: 418-665-3731
Rooms: 12 (8 with private bath; 4
share adjoining bath)
Rates: (M.A.P.) inexpensive
Credit Cards: MasterCard, Visa,
American Express
Facilities: Dining, swimming,
tennis. Closed October 15 to
December 15.

This newest star in the sky at Pointe-au-Pic was originally the 1890 summer home of an American, Mr Farnum. He would give grand parties every weekend in August to influential business and political guests. During these evenings, they watched the northern sky to view the dancing lights of the aurora borealis.

During one afternoon, I sat on the patio with Denys, having coffee. What a fantastic view of the river! Denys told me that those parties of old were so famous that when the inn first opened to the public in late 1982, the local people flocked around to share vicariously in the excitement.

Farnum kept the summer home until 1938 when he sold it to Charles Édouard Gravelle, the famous Quebec City financier. He used it as a summer residence until his death when his son, Louis, an architect and antique car buff, remodelled it in its present Mediterranean style.

Denys and Reine bought the building in 1982 and have created one of the most charming inns in the area. Each room is decorated individually and all have a glorious view of the river.

I was fortunate to eat dinner there. The dining room was very gracefully decorated with pink and royal blue napery. The table d'hôte meal I chose included a nice salad and a very delicate vegetable soup. The main course, a large portion of deliciously prepared roast beef, was a delight to the eye and palate. Other selections are the Lapereau Fondue with jeunes poireaux (young rabbit with leeks) and medallions of lotte (burbot). *Prices:* expensive.

Directions: Pointe-au-Pic is 150 kilometres (93 miles) east of Quebec City on Route 362, just off Route 138.

❖❖❖❖❖❖❖❖❖❖❖❖❖❖❖❖❖❖❖❖❖❖❖❖❖❖❖❖

Auberge des Peupliers

381, rue St-Raphael
Cap-à-l'Aigle, Québec
GoT 1Bo

Innkeeper: Ferdinand Tremblay
Telephone: 418-665-2519
Rooms: 21 (all with bath)
Rates: inexpensive
Credit Cards: MasterCard, Visa
Facilities: Dining, tennis, whirlpool, sauna. Open year-round.

I was fortunate to have Sunday brunch with Ferdinand. He exudes such a quiet charm, a charm born perhaps of three generations of inn-keeping. Sitting in the bright airy dining room, it was easy to enjoy the delicious brunch.

auberge des peupliers
cap-à-l'aigle, québec

Ferdinand has made very imaginative use of the barn, converting it to accommodations, all rooms with a great view of the river, and there is a sauna and whirlpool on the main floor. The original rustic charm of the barn has been kept by using the original beams and flooring.

The Sunday brunch offers homemade bread, buns, muffins, a delicious omelette with fine herbs, beans, bacon, salad bar, wine, dessert and coffee. The table d'hôte menu features the traditional Charlevoix dishes of lamb, salmon, scallops and smelts. *Prices:* expensive.

Many of the recipes have been handed down through the family and include pâté de foie gras and a dessert of delicious small cakes.

Directions: Cap-à-l'Aigle is on Route 138, about 145 kilometres east of Quebec City.

Auberge des Trois Canards

49, Côte Bellevue
Pointe-au-Pic, Québec
GoT 1Mo

Innkeepers: Claude and Pierre Marchand and Paul Couturier
Telephone: 418-665-3761
Rooms: 40 (all with bath)
Rates: moderate
Credit Cards: MasterCard, Visa, American Express
Facilities: Dining, tennis, outdoor pool. Open year-round.

Like many of his countrymen, Mr. Galt, a wealthy American, built what we know as The Auberge as a summer home in 1896. It remained a summer home until 1951, when it became a restaurant. In 1956, Paul, and later Claude and Pierre, converted the rooms in the house for public accommodation and added some motel units.

The prevalent legend has it that three prominent Quebec City doctors bought the place and, wishing anonymity, settled on the name The Three Docs. It later became Ducks, thus Trois Canards.

Whatever the origin, Paul and his colleagues have created a charming inn with a great view of the St. Lawrence. The room that particularly struck my fancy had a lovely porch where one could sit out and enjoy a drink and the scenery after a day of touring.

The three dining rooms serve a six-course table d'hôte dinner consisting of local Quebec lamb, beef, and fish. The favourites are scampis Provençale and medallions of beef. The choice dessert is the traditional sugar tart de la Bourgeoisie. *Prices:* expensive.

Directions: Pointe-au-Pic is 150 kilometres (93 miles) east of Quebec City on Route 362, just off Route 138.

❧❧❧❧❧❧❧❧❧❧❧❧❧❧❧❧❧❧❧❧❧❧❧❧❧❧❧❧❧❧❧❧❧

Auberge la Perdriole

278, rue Principale
St-Joseph-de-la-Rive,
Québec GoA 3Yo

Innkeeper: Catherine et Jean LeBlond
Telephone: 418-635-2435
Rooms: 14 (3 common baths)
Rates: inexpensive-to-moderate
Credit Cards: MasterCard, Visa
Facilities: Dining. Open January through October: Summer (Thursday to Sunday), Winter (Friday to Sunday). Also open during Christmas week.

Catherine's husband, Jean, is a jolly person who insisted on displaying his extensive wine list, something that is as much a source of pride to him as his modest inn. Modest, but very pleasing it is.

At the time of its inception as an inn in 1810, the river front was right at the door and the ships that used to ply the St. Lawrence often docked there. A stream used to run through the basement where there was a small mill. Horsedrawn wagons would bring the grain which was milled while they waited — a sort of drive-in mill.

The inn was under the ownership of the Boudreau family until 1960. In 1977, Catherine and Jean purchased it.

Perdriole is the poetic name for partridge and though Jean does not raise partridges on his half-hectare plot, he does raise lambs, pigs and cows. As well, he grows his own vegetables. Thus, the pièce de résistance of La Perdriole is the squash stuffed with lamb. Sometimes included on the table d'hôte menu, which changes daily, is Escalope de veau à la Normande, curried chicken and the traditional rabbit. *Prices:* expensive.

Directions: St-Joseph-de-la-Rive is just off Route 362, east of Baie St-Paul, about 110 kilometres (68 miles) from Quebec City.

❀❀❀❀❀❀❀❀❀❀❀❀❀❀❀❀❀❀❀❀❀❀

Auberge la Petite Marmite

63, rue Principale
Pointe-au-Pic, Québec
GoT 1Mo

Innkeepers: Danielle Amyot and Danielle Belley
Telephone: 418-665-3583
Rooms: 7 (4 with bath)
Rates: (M.A.P.) moderate
Credit Cards: MasterCard, Visa
Facilities: Dining, swimming. Open all year-round.

The front porch of La Petite Marmite should have an historic plaque. For there (as it is told), the Union Nationale was formed, back in the 1930s, on a handshake between Antonio Talbot and Maurice Duplessis. It is rather appropriate that a political event took place there, for in the late 1800s it was the summer home of Albert Sévigny, a Supreme Court judge. As a matter of fact, Sévigny's granddaughters visit the inn quite frequently.

On asking the two Danielles my usual question about ghosts, they told me that the Sévigny girls were warned by their mother not to go into the third-floor room behind the sewing room because of the ghosts. To date, no ghosts have been found and it is suspected that the mother simply did not want the girls to disturb her sewing.

This very comfortable, old Victorian home has lovely bedrooms and the living room has a lovely view of the St. Lawrence.

The table d'hôte meal features a typical Charlevoix recipe from a fishing guide called Fricassée of Trout. Also included is Filet of Sole Meunière and Escalope of Veal Milanaise. *Prices:* expensive.

Directions: Pointe-au-Pic is 150 kilometres (93 miles) east of Quebec City on Route 362, just off Route 138.

AUBERGE
LA
Pinsonnière

Auberge la Pinsonnière

124, rue St-Raphael
Cap-à-l'Aigle, Québec
GoT 1Bo

Innkeepers: Janine and Jean Authier
Telephone: 418-665-3272
Rooms: 23 (15 with bath)
Rates: (M.A.P.) moderate
Credit Cards: Master Card, Visa
Facilities: Dining. Private Beach.
Open year-round.

A *pinsonnière* is a sparrow's nest, and the name is used to symbolize the peace and quiet of the countryside. When I dropped in to see Jean and Janine, the chirping of the sparrows was being drowned out by the whine of saws and the blows of hammers. They were in the process of adding a continuous unit of 12 suites to the original building. The architecture of the new section will blend in perfectly with the old house and every room will have a great view of the river.

As is not uncommon among Quebec inns, the original building was destroyed by fire, this one in 1944. It had been built at the turn of the century as a summer home for a wealthy American. Later, it was sold to Oscar Drouin, a minister in the Duplessis government. The house also once belonged to a Mr. Dempsey, who at one time owned the nearby Manoir Richelieu.

Jean took me downstairs to show me the wine cellar, his pride and joy. According to him, he has one of the top 25 wine cellars in the province with wines ranging from $13.75 to $500.00 a bottle. Perhaps the most unusual item on the table d'hôte menu is the Pintadine et sa Farce aux Raisins. This wild bird is stuffed with bread and grapes before being roasted. Other items on the menu reflect the Charlevoix setting: smelts, salmon and rabbit. I noticed a dessert, le Pouding au Pain Suprème. Originally this dessert was called Pouding au Chômeur, pudding for the unemployed or poor. It is a delicious dessert that has certainly been fancied up from its humble beginnings. *Prices:* expensive.

Directions: Cap-à-l'Aigle is on Route 138, about 145 kilometres east of Quebec City.

❧❧❧❧❧❧❧❧❧❧❧❧❧❧❧❧❧❧❧❧❧

Auberge la Rose au Bois

169, boulevard des Falaises
Pointe-au-Pic, Québec
GoT 1Mo

Innkeeper: Jean-Paul Bernier
Telephone: 418-665-6796
Rooms: 10 (6 with bath)
Rates: very inexpensive
Credit Cards: All major cards
Facilities: Dining. Golf, tennis, cross-country and downhill skiing nearby.

One evening during my stay at Pointe-au-Pic, I dropped into the Auberge to find Jean-Paul tending bar. He greeted me warmly. He proudly showed me around his inn claiming that the difference between an innkeeper and hotelier is that an innkeeper is clever enough to keep his place small.

Jean-Paul took over this 1847 restaurant with its charming rooms and balconies overlooking the bay in 1973. It is the oldest existing inn in Pointe-au-Pic and was originally the private residence for Lady Harris of Boston. Later, A.T. Galt of the Grand Trunk Railway owned it.

As we sat out on the comfortable closed-in porch, I noticed a young couple playing backgammon next to me. This characterizes the low-key atmosphere of the inn. I asked Jean-Paul the significance

of the inn's name. "We have a walled-in garden with wild roses," he said.

Jean-Paul boasts a very extensive table d'hôte menu which includes his favourites: quail with grapes in wine sauce, trout stuffed with crab and salmon, the traditional Quebec rabbit with mustard sauce, and steak with peppers or cognac sauce. One of the desserts unique to the Auberge is a cake with preserves fashioned like the petals of a rose. *Prices:* expensive.

Directions: Pointe-au-Pic is 150 kilometres (93 miles) east of Quebec City on Route 362, just off Route 138.

❖❖❖❖❖❖❖❖❖❖❖❖❖❖❖❖❖❖❖❖❖❖❖

Auberge les Sources

8, avenue des Pins
Pointe-au-Pic, Québec
GoT 1Mo

Innkeeper: Hugues de Merlis
Telephone: 418-665-6952
Rooms: 20 (18 with bath)
Rates: (M.A.P.) moderate
Credit Cards: MasterCard, Visa
Facilities: Dining. Tennis, swimming, golf, fishing, skiing nearby. Closed October 15 to December 20.

In the early part of the century, Les Sources was built as a summer home for a Mr. Jones, a wealthy American citizen. In the 1930s, a Mr. Amyot bought it. He was the wealthy scion of a family which operated a clothing factory in Quebec City.

The Merlis purchased the home in 1974, after moving from their native Saskatchewan, and, in 1977, they turned it into a lovely inn. Auberge Les Sources was named for the nearby spring that supplies all the table water. No need to order Perrier there. Each room is distinctively furnished, some with glassed-in balconies, sitting rooms and fireplaces. And, of course, they all have the most prized possession of all — a great view of the river.

The menu features Fantaisies de l'Aubergiste: cubes of Filet Mignon with ginger, trout with local garlic, and mousse of sole on bread with crab. Other items include mignon of pork, twelve-ounce steak with choice of peppers and grilled scallops. *Prices:* moderate.

Directions: Pointe-au-Pic is 150 kilometres (93 miles) east of Quebec City on Route 362, just off Route 138.

❖❖❖❖❖❖❖❖❖❖❖❖❖❖❖❖❖❖❖❖❖❖❖❖❖❖

Hôtel Cap aux Pierres

220 est, Route Principale
Île-aux-Coudres, La-Baleine
Québec G0A 2A0

Innkeepers: The Dufour Family
Telephone: 418-438-2711
Rooms: 90 (A.P.)
Rates: moderate
Credit Cards: MasterCard, Visa, American Express
Facilities: Dining, indoor and outdoor pools, sauna, badminton, tennis, cross-country skiing. Open year-round.

When I walked into the lobby of the Hôtel Cap aux Pierres, I noticed the Dufour family coat of arms above the fireplace. I learned that the basic part of the coat of arms goes back to the family's origins in Normandy where the Dufours held a seigneury near the seashore. The crescent and light-coloured bar across the top represent the sandy shore and are set off against the three silver stars in the azure blue sky.

When the Dufour family came to Canada with 18 other colonists in 1725 to take up a seigneury on the island, they added the wreath of hazelnuts to show the link with their fellow-Norman, Jacques Cartier, who named the island after the hazelnuts he found growing here in 1535.

Since then, twelve generations of the Dufour family have prospered on the island, and their ancestral family home is nearby. The more recent descendants of the family set up their family home at the inn in 1956 and, as seems to have been the pattern in Quebec, started taking in the many guests that flooded Charlevoix and l'Île-aux-Coudres. A disastrous fire levelled the home in 1976 but it was rebuilt to become the comfortable country inn and motel now overlooking Cap aux Pierres and the St. Lawrence.

My dinner consisted of local fresh halibut nicely prepared and served. *Prices:* moderate.

Directions: From St-Joseph-de-la-Rive (110 kilometres (68 miles) east of Quebec City, off Route 362), take a pleasant 15-minute ferry ride across the St. Lawrence to Île-aux-Coudres.

Hôtel Georges

135, rue du Bateau-Passeur
Tadoussac, Québec
GoT 2Ao

Innkeeper: Langis Lessard
Telephone: 418-235-4393
Rooms: 21, 11 with bath
Rates: very inexpensive
Credit Cards: MasterCard, Visa
Facilities: Dining for 35 people.
Licensed. Whale-sighting from
hotel balcony. Open year-round.

As I crossed the Saguenay to reach Tadoussac (a short ferry ride), I looked up the river to view huge granite cliffs rising steeply toward magnificent forests as far as the eye could see. I wondered what the explorers, Cartier and Champlain, must have thought as they viewed this same sight on their first sailing trips down the St. Lawrence. What promise this vast landscape must have held for them!

It was here that William Price, founder of Price Lumber Company, built a home for his family in 1839. The Prince of Wales stopped by, at the invitation of the Prices, to enjoy the famous Saguenay salmon fishing in 1860. After the home became an inn in 1905, visitors included a future Governor General, Georges Vanier.

The house has since been enlarged and motel units added to accommodate the many guests who visit the Saguenay area. One of the nicest features of the hotel is the glassed-in porch overlooking the river. It serves as a dining lounge during the summer.

The dining menu features a wide variety of seafood, including scampis and Coquille St-Jacques. Also available are pepper steak, ham with pineapple and veal liver with bacon. *Prices:* moderate.

Directions: Tadoussac is 200 kilometres (124 miles) east of Quebec City on Route 138.

Hôtel Tadoussac

165, rue Bord de l'Eau
Tadoussac, Québec
GoT 2Ao

Innkeepers: Antoine Perroud and Georges Python
Telephone: 418-235-4421
Rooms: 127, most with bath
Rates: (European Plan) inexpensive
Credit Cards: All major cards
Facilities: Dining, tennis, beach and pool swimming. Open May 1 to September 30.

William Hugh Cloverdale, one-time president of Canada Steamship Lines and builder of the original Hôtel Tadoussac, was also a writer. In his *Tadoussac, Then and Now*, he writes of the settlement's origin three centuries before. In 1600, the first stockade/trading post in the colony was built just beside the hotel's present location by Pierre Chauvin de Honfleur, who was granted a ten-year, fur-trading monopoly by Henry IV of France. Cloverdale writes of the development of the Saguenay River region and its eventual change from a fur-trading area to an industrial centre with a huge aluminum smelter located upstream at Arvida.

Originally part of the shipping empire put together by Cloverdale, the hotel served travellers sailing from Toronto, down the St. Lawrence and then up the Saguenay. When the boats stopped running, Cloverdale sold the hotel. It still stands overlooking the magnificent Saguenay, a typical Victorian summer hotel with white clapboards set off by a bright red roof. This gracious building is surrounded by a great wide lawn strewn with patio and lawn chairs for comfortable summer lounging. Also typical of the Victorian hotel is the screened-in porch housing a summer bar and dining area.

According to the innkeeper, Antoine Perroud, the favourites of the menu are Brochettes of beef, ribsteak with pepper sauce and Filet Mignon. *Prices:* moderate.

Directions: Tadoussac is 200 kilometres (124 miles) east of Quebec City on Route 138.

❧❧❧❧❧❧❧❧❧❧❧❧❧❧❧❧❧❧❧❧❧❧❧❧❧

La Maison Donohue

145, rue Principale
Pointe-au-Pic, Québec
G0T 1M0

Innkeepers: Monique and Orval Aumont
Telephone: 418-665-4377
Rooms: 7 (six with bath)
Rates: moderate
Credit Cards: MasterCard, Visa
Facilities: Outdoor pool. Open year-round.

The most imposing feature of La Maison is the stone turret that corners the house and rises two floors to the top of the building. Inside, the main floor is a huge living room with a grand fireplace, comfortable furniture, tables and all kinds of board and card games for a relaxing evening. The wood ceiling has beams radiating from the centre. Up the beautiful winding staircase, the turret houses the master bedroom decorated with fine, bright Victorian furniture and offering a magnificent view of the St. Lawrence.

Tommy Donohue, the owner of Donohue Paper in nearby Clermont, built La Maison as a summer home in the early 1900s to entertain friends and business acquaintances. Designed by the architect Charles Warren, whose magic can be seen in many of the fine summer homes in the area, it passed through the family until 1970 when a well-known Quebec City lawyer bought the house, also as a summer residence.

In 1979, Orval and Monique, completely enchanted by Charlevoix country, decided to buy the home and turn it into an auberge. Working night and day, they transformed 11 rooms into seven very comfortable and luxurious bedrooms. They also fixed up a summer cottage on the property to accommodate families.

Monique and Orval do not serve meals but provide a sumptuous breakfast of juice, coffee, croissants, doughnuts and fresh fruit.

Directions: Pointe-au-Pic is 150 kilometres (93 miles) east of Quebec City on Route 362, just off Route 138.

La Maison Otis

23, rue St-Jean Baptiste
Baie St-Paul, Québec
G0A 1B0

Innkeepers: Jean-Baptiste Bouchard
and Michel Villeneuve
Telephone: 418-435-2255
Rooms: 18 (all with bath)
Rates: (M.A.P.) inexpensive-to-
expensive
Credit Cards: MasterCard, Visa
Facilities: Dining, skiing, whirlpool.
Closed in November.

Jean and Michel are two young men who have taken this fine old building on the main street of Baie St-Paul and created an establishment with ultra-chic sophistication that retains its historical integrity.

Adolphe Gagnon, mayor of St-Paul and a deputy in the National Assembly, took fourteen years to build this home, completing it in 1836, but he never actually lived in it. Later, it became the first Provin-

cial Bank in the area. Its vault now protects the inn's fine wine. It also became the City Hall for a time and eventually took its name from its last residents, the Otis family.

The property was slated for demolition but Michel and Jean rescued it, much to the relief of the people of Baie St-Paul. No sooner had renovations started when a disastrous fire gutted the interior. Fortunately, the thick stone walls withstood the heat and the restoration was finally completed with a great deal of grace and beauty. They also bought the building next door, an historic schoolhouse with two classrooms upstairs.

Their creativity is amazing — no room is the same. Some suites have two floors; others have a whirlpool; and all of them have a stunning décor. All rooms are named after local notable families of the area — Tremblay, Boivin, Bouchard.

I was fortunate to arrive for lunch. I enjoyed a plate of fresh vegetables, vichyssoise, and a crisp croissant with ham and cheese, cake and coffee.

Michel tells me that they concentrate on Quebec cuisine — pheasant with grapes, trout, filet of sole, rabbit in mustard sauce, and escalope of salmon. *Prices:* expensive.

Directions: Baie St-Paul is 80 kilometres (50 miles) east of Quebec City on Route 138.

❧❧❧❧❧❧❧❧❧❧❧❧❧❧❧❧❧❧❧❧❧❧❧❧❧❧

Le Club des Monts

85, rang Ruisseau des Frênes
Ste-Agnace, Québec
GoT 1Co

Innkeeper: Christianne Marchand
Telephone: 418-439-3711
Credit Cards: MasterCard, Visa
Facilities: Dining. No liquor (bring your own wine). Open every day at 6 p.m. (June 1 to October 10). Reservations only.

It seems that Nore Sellar, an American summer resident, owned a home near St-Siméon, some twenty miles distant. This was formerly the private residence of an unknown person some hundred years ago. Suddenly, in 1937, Sellar decided he was going to move the building piece by piece to Ste-Agnace and turn it into a restaurant — Le Club des Monts.

Christianne took me on a tour of Le Club and showed me doors that disappeared, doors that opened into bookcases, halls so narrow one had to walk sideways, and floors with board games printed in the linoleum. After showing me all this, Christianne turned to me and said to me in what must be the understatement of the century, "Mr. Sellar was slightly eccentric."

Mr Sellar ran the restaurant until he died in 1974. The building remained vacant until recently when Christianne (her husband is inn-keeper at Les Trois Canards in Pointe-au-Pic) bought the place, pledging to continue the Sellar tradition of serving excellent steaks.

I was seated at a plain wooden table in a room illuminated only by candles. All the tables were covered with inscriptions by former guests who, like the guests today, were offered a hammer and nail to pound out their name and date. Many guests bring their children to show them where they, as younger people, had inscribed their names. As further decoration, all the beams are covered with business cards of guests dating back to 1937.

Yes, Mr. Sellar was a little eccentric.

However, there was nothing odd about the meal I was served. It began with a very good onion soup with cheese. Then, of course, came la pièce de résistance, a one-pound T-bone steak barbecued perfectly with fried onions and some delicious mashed potatoes. For dessert I was served a cooked orange in which was injected some non-alcoholic mint liqueur — delicious. *Prices:* expensive.

Directions: From Pointe-au-Pic take Route 138 for 16 kilometres to Ste-Agnace and then follow the signs to Le Club.

❖❖❖❖❖❖❖❖❖❖❖❖❖❖❖❖❖❖❖❖❖❖❖❖❖

Manoir Charlevoix

1030, rue St-Étienne
La Malbaie, Québec
GoT 1Jo

Innkeeper: François Savard
Telephone: 418-665-4413
Rooms: 42 (all with bath)
Rates: (M.A.P.) moderate
Credit Cards: MasterCard, Visa, American Express
Facilities: Dining. Outdoor pool, sauna, tennis. Open all year-round.

Over a cup of coffee in the pine-beamed dining room, François Savard recounted the history of the inn as documented by the

Museum of La Malbaie. This museum, by the way, has as one of its features a section devoted to the research of the history of tourism in Charlevoix, an indication of how important the tourist industry is to that section of the country.

In 1868, Jean-Olivier Chamard rented the Riverside House as an inn to attract wealthy tourists from Montreal and the U.S. In 1872, he named the house Chamard's Lorne House in honour of the Marquis of Lorne who later became Canada's Governor General. Reputed to be not a manor but a "state of mind", Lorne House attracted such distinguished visitors as William Howard Taft, 27th President of the United States, as well as travellers from as far away as Virginia and Ohio.

In 1901, the current Manoir was constructed on the site, bolted to the cliff. It offers a stunning view of the St. Lawrence.

François says that the favourites of the table d'hôte menu are the filet of pork with apple sauce, escalope of veal in cream sauce and scampis au Manoir. Other items include a ten-ounce steak in wine sauce, veal liver and salmon steak with hollandaise sauce. *Prices:* expensive.

Directions: La Malbaie is about 150 kilometres (93 miles) east of Quebec City on Route 138.

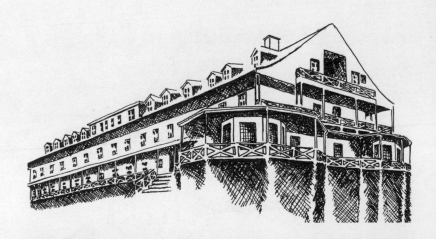

Manoir Richelieu

181, avenue Richelieu
Pointe-au-Pic, Québec
GoT 1Mo

Innkeepers: The Dufour family
Telephone: 418-665-3703
Rooms: 333
Rates: (M.A.P.) moderate-to-expensive
Credit Cards: All major cards
Facilities: Dining, tennis, badminton, outdoor pool. Golf, boating, alpine and cross-country skiing nearby.

I used the Manoir as a base for my travels in Charlevoix country and in my comings and goings I was constantly searching my mind for a word that would capture the essence of the inn. Each evening, the lobby would be filled with crowds of people surrounding a piano player and belting out Québécois songs with unrestrained joy.

As I entered my room and opened the window I noticed a little sign on the sill which said in part in English, "Please do not place articles on the window sill —". This was the notice left over from the old days when English was the only language of the Manoir, when Francophones dared not set foot inside the hallowed English halls. Today, the Manoir is owned by the Quebec Government and the guests are truly, joyfully "maître chez nous". Now people from all over the world flock to see the wonders of Charlevoix and "le Manoir".

The history of the Manoir goes back almost 200 years when rich American families began to build their summer homes in beautiful Charlevoix country. Among them were President Taft of the United States and many of his friends. In 1899, the steamship company that was to become Canada Steamship Lines built the Manoir as one of its major stopping places on voyages up the St. Lawrence from Toronto. They would pick up wealthy guests from Montreal and Quebec who often spent the whole summer at the Manoir.

A disastrous fire in 1928 burned down the building but, fortunately, it was rebuilt under the guidance of its owner, Mr. Cloverdale, and architect John Archibald. It was fashioned in the manner of old Scottish castles with impressive granite walls and *bâtiments* with copper roofing. Of course, the grounds are magnificent and the view of the St. Lawrence is outstanding.

The rooms are built in the old style, large and comfortable with very high ceilings and old-fashioned furniture.

After the Canada Steamship Lines stopped serving the area in 1966, the inn began its downward slide to bankruptcy in 1976. At that point, the Government of Quebec took it over and awarded the management contract to Auberge des Gouverneurs. Now, it is proudly run by the Dufour family who also own Hôtel Cap aux Pierres on l'Île-aux-Coudres.

Directions: Pointe-au-Pic is 150 kilometres (93 miles) east of Quebec City on Route 362, just off Route 138.

Index